*Conversational*

# SPANISH

## IN 7 DAYS

SHIRLEY BALDWIN & SARAH BOAS

**PASSPORT BOOKS**
a division of *NTC Publishing Group*
Lincolnwood, Illinois USA

# ACKNOWLEDGMENTS

The authors and publishers are grateful to the following for supplying photographs:

Barnaby's Picture Library: (pp. 9, 21, 30, 59)
J. Allan Cash Ltd: (Cover, pp. 1, 6, 7, 12, 16, 18, 19, 23, 24, 26, 34, 38, 40, 47, 50, 53, 57, 62, 67, 71)
D.J. Fox: (pp. 30, 42, 55)

**Photo credits**

front cover:
*top*   Tourism Division, Texas Department of Commerce
*middle*   National Tourism Office of Spain
*bottom*   Chip Peterson and Rosa María de la Cueva Peterson

back cover: National Tourism Office of Spain

**1996 Printing**

This edition first published in 1991 by Passport Books,
a division of NTC Publishing Group,
4255 West Touhy Avenue, Lincolnwood (Chicago),
Illinois 60646-1975. Originally published by Hodder & Stoughton Publishers.
© Shirley Baldwin and Sarah Boas, 1988. All rights reserved.
No part of this book may be reproduced, stored in a retrieval system, or
transmitted in any form, or by any means, electronic, mechanical, photocopying,
or otherwise, without the prior permission of NTC Publishing Group.
Printed in Hong Kong.

6 7 8 9 0 WKT 9 8

# CONTENTS

# INTRODUCTION

**Conversational Spanish in 7 Days** is a short course in Spanish which will equip you to deal with everyday situations when you visit a Spanish-speaking country: shopping, eating out, asking for directions, changing money, and so on.

The course is divided into 7 units, each corresponding to a day in the life of Carmen (a journalist), her husband Tom, and their two teenage children during their week in Spain. Each unit begins with a dialogue, which introduces the essential language items in context. Key phrases are highlighted in the dialogues, and the phrasebook section which follows lists these and other useful phrases and tells you what they are in English.

Within the units there are also short information sections in English on the topics covered, sections giving basic grammatical explanations, and a number of follow-up activities designed to be useful as well as fun. Answers can be checked in a key at the back of the book. Also available with this program are 2 cassettes to help you practice your Spanish.

## *Pronunciation*

**1** Pronounce each part of every word; Spanish sounds very much as it is written.
**2** Emphasize the second-to-last syllable of every word which ends with a vowel or **n** or **s**.
**3** Emphasize the last syllable of every word which ends in a consonant other than **n** or **s**. (Exceptions to these rules carry a written accent.)

**Vowels:** do not vary their sounds as in English:

a as *a* in *father*; la, mamá
e as in *next*; este, señor
i as *ee* in *meek*; mi, marido
  Before another vowel:
  like **y**; día [deeya], bien
o as in *go*; coche, como

u as *oo* in *moose*; lunes, mucho
  Before another vowel or **y**:
  like **w**; bueno [bwehno], muy [mwee]
  After **q** and in **gue/gui**:
  u is silent; aquí [akee], seguida

**Consonants:** similar to English but with the following exceptions:

b  Between vowels:
   almost **v**; bebida, trabajo
c  Before **a, o, u**:
   like *kilo*; como, coche
   Before **e, i**:
   like *thanks*; gracias, hace
ch like *chair*; mucho, chico
d  Between vowels & at end of words:
   almost like *th*; seguida, verdad
g  Before **a, o, u**: like *gap*; gusto
   Before **e, i**: like *henna*; general

h  always silent; hija, hotel
j  like *ham*; hija, ajo
ll like *yolk*; llamo [yahmo]
ñ  like *onion*; señor, señora
qu like *kilo*; que, aquí
r  always sounded, sometimes rolled: verdad
rr strongly rolled: correos, corrida
s  like *sun*; sí, soy
v  mixture of **b** and **v**; vamos
z  like *thank*; plaza, zapato

# SAYING HELLO

▶ **Arrival**  When arriving in Spain, you will find customs (**Aduana**) and passport procedures standard and easy to follow, because most information is given in English as well as Spanish.

## mucho gusto/pleased to meet you

Carmen Roberts, a Spanish journalist working in London, has been sent to Madrid to research a story. She is with her husband, Tom, and their two children, Luisa and Miguel. The family is met in Madrid by Andrés Valbuena, a fellow journalist.

| | |
|---|---|
| Andrés: | **Hola. Buenos días. ¿Es usted la señora Roberts, por favor?** |
| Carmen: | **Sí, soy** Carmen Roberts. **¿Cómo se llama usted?** |
| Andrés: | **Me llamo** Andrés Valbuena. **Encantado**, señora Roberts. |
| Carmen: | **Encantada**. Le presento a mi marido, Tom. |
| Andrés: | **Mucho gusto, señor.** |
| Carmen: | **Y esta es mi hija**, Luisa, y este (sees Miguel looking at some magazines) es mi hijo. ¡Miguel, venga! Vamos en coche con el señor Valbuena. |

1

On the way to the office, Luisa and Miguel are dropped off at their aunt's apartment. Luisa is greeted by Juan, her 19-year-old Spanish cousin.

Juan:     ¡Hola! ¿Qué tal, Luisa?
Luisa:     **Muy bien, ¿y tú, cómo estás?**
Juan:     Pues, **bien, gracias**. ¡Hola, Miguel! ¿Qué tal?
Miguel:     Bien, gracias.
Juan:     Dame tus maletas. (He picks up the suitcases)
Luisa:     **Gracias**, primo, eres muy amable.
Juan:     **De nada**.
Luisa:     Y tu madre, ¿cómo está?
Juan:     Mi madre está bien. (Calls) ¡Mamá! Aquí están Luisa y Miguel.
Pilar:     ¡Hola! ¡Qué bien, Luisa y Miguel!

### Saying hello

| | |
|---|---|
| **Hola. Buenos días.** | Hello. Good morning. |
| **Buenas tardes.** | Good afternoon./Good evening. |
| **Buenas noches.** | Good evening./Good night. |

**Addressing people in Spanish**    In Spanish you address a man as **señor** (Mr.), a woman as **señora** (Mrs.), and a girl or young unmarried woman as **señorita** (Miss). It is normal to shake hands both when meeting someone for the first time and also when saying *Hello* or *Goodbye* to a friend or acquaintance. Note that there is a formal and informal way of saying "you." Use the formal **usted** form (the third person of the verb) until you know somebody well, then change to the **tú** form (the second person). In the family and among friends and younger people, the informal form is very frequently used.

### Meeting people

| | |
|---|---|
| **¿Cómo se llama usted?** | What's your name? (formal) |
| **¿Cómo te llamas?** | What's your name? (informal) |
| **Me llamo . . ./Soy . . .** | My name is . . ./I am . . . |
| **¿Cómo se llama?** | What's his/her name? |
| **Se llama . . .** | His/her name is . . . |
| **¿Es usted la señora Valbuena?** | Are you Mrs. Valbuena? |
| **Este es . . . (mi hijo)** | This is . . . (my son) |
| **Esta es . . . (mi hija)** | This is . . . (my daughter) |
| **Le presento a . . .** | May I introduce you to . . . (formal) |
| **. . . mi esposa, mi marido** | . . . my wife, my husband |
| **. . . mi amigo, mi amiga** | . . . my friend |
| **Te presento a . . .** | Let me introduce you to . . . (informal) |
| **Encantado./Encantada.** | Pleased to meet you. (said by a man/a woman) |
| **Mucho gusto./Tanto gusto.** | Pleased to meet you. |

## Asking how someone is

| | |
|---|---|
| ¿Cómo está usted? | How are you? (formal) |
| Muy bien, gracias, ¿y usted? | Very well, thank you, and you? |
| ¿Cómo estás? | How are you? (informal) |
| ¿Qué tal? ¿Qué hay? | How are things? How's it going? |
| Muy bien, ¿y tú? | Fine (thanks), and you? |
| Bien. | O.K. |
| ¿Cómo está? | How is he/she? |
| Está bien. | He/she is well. |

## Yes and No

Sí/No    Yes/No

## Saying please and thank you

| | |
|---|---|
| Por favor/Gracias | Please/Thank you |
| Muchas gracias. | Thank you very much. |
| Eres muy amable. | You are very kind. (informal) |
| De nada./No hay de qué. | You're welcome./Don't mention it. |

## OTHER USEFUL PHRASES

| | |
|---|---|
| ¡Venga! | Come here! |
| Vamos en coche | We are going by car |
| con el señor Valbuena | with Mr. Valbuena |
| Dame tu maleta. | Give me your suitcase. |
| Tu madre/Mi madre | Your mother/My mother |
| ¡Qué bien! | How nice! |

## the way it works

### People and things

In Spanish words for both people and things are said to be either masculine or feminine. The word for "the" is:
**el** for a masculine word: **el** señor (man), **el** coche (car);
**la** for a feminine word: **la** señora (lady), **la** maleta (suitcase).
Most words ending in **-o** are masculine (**el** hijo = son, **el** marido = husband) and most words ending in **-a** are feminine (**la** esposa = wife, **la** maleta = suitcase). But there are several other endings and it is a good idea to learn each word together with **el** or **la**, e.g., el coche = car (**-e** is usually masculine). Don't worry if you get it wrong. You'll usually be understood!

### To make a word plural

**El** becomes **los**, and **la** becomes **las**. The ending of the word changes: add **-s** to words ending in a vowel and **-es** to words ending in a consonant: e.g., **las** maletas (the suitcases), **los** señores (the men).

## Who are you?/What are you?

**Soy** Carmen Roberts.  I am Carmen Roberts.
**Eres** muy amable.  You are very kind.
**¿Es** usted el señor Valbuena?  Are you Mr. Valbuena?
You will see that there are two verbs in Spanish meaning "to be." The one we'll learn first is **ser**. Here is the pattern of its present tense:

| singular | | | plural | | |
|---|---|---|---|---|---|
| (yo) | **soy** | I am | (nosotros) | **somos** | we are |
| (tú) | **eres** | you are (informal) | (vosotros) | **sois** | you are |
| (él/ella) | **es** | he/she/it is | (ellos/ellas) | **son** | they are |
| (usted) | **es** | you are (formal | (ustedes) | **son** | you are (formal) |

Use this verb for saying who you are and for describing permanent qualities.

## Subject pronouns

**Yo** (I), **tú, usted** (you), **él** (he) etc. are *subject pronouns*. Because the ending of the verb shows who is the subject, you do not normally need to use these except to avoid ambiguity or to emphasize the subject.

## How are you?/Where are you?

¿Como **estás**?  How are you?
**Estoy** muy bien. I am very well.

The second verb meaning "to be" is **estar**.
Here is the pattern of its endings:

| **estoy** | I am | **estamos** | we are |
|---|---|---|---|
| **estás** | you are | **estáis** | you are |
| **está** | he/she is | **están** | they are |
| **está** | you are (formal) | **están** | you are (formal) |

Use this verb for asking how someone is and for talking about where something or somebody is:

Aquí **está** Luisa.  Here is Luisa.
¿Dónde **están?**  Where are they?

## My/your/his

There are several examples of these possessive adjectives in the Dialogues: **mi** esposa, **mi** hijo, **mi** hija, **tus** maletas, **tu** madre. The full list is as follows:

| **mi/mis** | my | **nuestro(s)/nuestra(s)** | our |
|---|---|---|---|
| **tu/tus** | your (informal) | **vuestro(s)/vuestra(s)** | your (informal) (when |
| **su/sus** | your (formal); his/her/ | | talking to more than |
| | its/their | | one person) |

*Note:* The possessive adjective agrees in gender and number *with the word it accompanies*, not with the possessor.

## Exclamations

**¡Hola!** Hello!  **¡Venga!** Come here!  **¡Qué bien!** How nice!

In written Spanish you always put an inverted exclamation mark at the beginning as well as the normal one at the end.

## Asking questions and saying No

Asking a question is very simple. There are several alternative methods:

**Question:**  ¿Es usted la señora Roberts? (subject pronoun after verb)
¿Usted es la señora Roberts? (same word order, rising intonation)
Usted es la señora Roberts, ¿verdad? (no change of word order but add
      **¿verdad?** or **¿no?** = isn't it? etc)
**Statement:** Sí, soy Carmen Roberts.

In written Spanish you always put an inverted question mark at the beginning of every question as well as the normal one at the end.
**Negative statement:** Insert **no** immediately before the verb.
No, no soy Carmen Roberts.    I am not Carmen Roberts.

## things to do

**1.1**  Carmen is meeting a lot of people. Some of them she knows already:
José Machado, elderly business colleague of her husband:
Buenos días, señor. [She asks him how he is]
¿Cómo está usted?
  **1** Mrs. Valbuena, wife of the journalist:
    [She says good morning and asks her how she is]
  **2** Mr. Gómez, business contact:
    [She says good afternoon, and asks him how he is]
  **3** Luis Ferrer, an old friend:
    [She says hello and asks him how he is]
    He says: Estoy muy bien, gracias, ¿y tú, cómo estás?
    [She says that she is well]
  **4** Mari-Carmen Alfonso, her daughter's friend:
    [She says hello, good afternoon, and asks how things are]

**1.2**  Annie Rogers has arrived with her brother (**su hermano**) for a visit to a Spanish family. What does she say to the customs officer?
Aduanero:  Su pasaporte, por favor. ¿Es usted la señorita Rogers?
Annie:  .................................................
Aduanero:  Este es su hermano, ¿verdad?
Annie:  .................................................
Aduanero:  ¿Es ésta su maleta?
Annie:  .................................................
Aduanero:  Y ¿ésta es la maleta de su hermano?
Annie:  .................................................
Aduanero:  Muy bien, señorita, gracias.

**1.3**  Make up questions for the following answers:
  **1** Sí, soy la señora Barillo.   **4** Estoy muy bien, gracias.
  **2** No, no es mi maleta.     **5** Mi hermana se llama María Teresa.
  **3** Está en la oficina.

# MAKING CONVERSATION

## ¿cómo es tu casa?/what's your house like?

Juan plans to take Luisa and Miguel to their vacation house near Santander.

Luisa: **¿Dónde está tu casa?**
Juan: **Está cerca de Santander.**
Luisa: ¿Cómo es la casa? **¿Es grande?**
Juan: **No, es bastante pequeña.** Hay dos cuartos de dormir, un cuarto de estar, un comedor, una cocina moderna, un cuarto de baño y también hay una terraza y un jardín.
Luisa: ¿Está cerca del mar?
Juan: Sí, está muy cerca y hay una vista maravillosa de la playa.
Luisa: ¡Estupendo! **¿Y cuándo vamos?**
Juan: Pues, **¿vamos el miércoles?**
Luisa: De acuerdo. El miércoles está bien. ¿Vamos en tren?
Juan: Sí. Vamos en tren a Santander.

### About the house

| | |
|---|---|
| **¿Dónde está tu casa?** | Where is your house? |
| **Está cerca de . . .** | It's near . . . |
| **¿Cómo es la casa?** | What's the house like? |
| **grande, pequeño/a** | big, small |
| **Hay/tiene** | There is, there are/it has |
| dos dormitorios | two bedrooms |
| un cuarto de estar | a living room |
| un comedor | a dining room |

| | |
|---|---|
| una cocina moderna | a modern kitchen |
| un cuarto de baño | a bathroom |
| una terraza, un jardín | a terrace, a garden |
| Está muy cerca del mar. | It's very near the sea. |
| Hay una vista maravillosa de la playa. | There is a wonderful view of the beach. |

### Days of the week

| | |
|---|---|
| ¿Cuándo vamos? | When shall we go? |
| Vamos el miércoles. | We'll go on Wednesday. |
| El miércoles está bien. | Wednesday is fine. |

### OTHER USEFUL PHRASES

| | | | | | |
|---|---|---|---|---|---|
| muy | very | también | too, also | De acuerdo. | Agreed, O.K. |
| bastante | quite, enough | ¡Estupendo! | Great! | Vamos en tren. | We'll go by train. |

# ORDERING DRINKS AND SNACKS

▷ **Spanish bars**   Spanish bars are crowded and friendly places and offer a wide variety of drinks and food. You can choose to stand at the counter (**la barra**) or sit at a table, or sometimes on the terrace (**terraza**), where you can watch the world go by but will pay a bit more. Although service will have been included, it is customary to give an extra tip (5%–10%) or at least to give some small change, if you are pleased with the service.

Many bars serve food as well. Often you will find rows of small dishes of appetizers (**tapas**) skewered with toothpicks laid out on the counter. If you want one of these, ask for **un pincho**. Larger portions are called **raciones**, and you will find there is often a huge variety to choose from.

## vamos a tomar una copa/let's have a drink

Before supper the family decides to pay a visit to a nearby bar.

| | |
|---|---|
| Camarero: | Buenas tardes, señores. ¿Qué van a tomar? |
| Carmen: | Miguel, tú, ¿qué tomas? |
| Miguel: | **Una coca-cola, por favor.** |
| Carmen: | **Y para mí un vermut.** Con hielo y limón, por favor. ¿Y tú, Luisa? |
| Luisa: | **Quiero** un zumo de naranja, por favor. |
| Camarero: | Sí, señorita. |
| Tom: | Yo quiero un vaso de vino tinto, por favor. |
| Camarero: | Muy bien, señores. ¿Quieren algo para comer? |
| Carmen: | **¿Qué tapas hay?** |
| Camarero: | Hay anchoas, aceitunas, calamares fritos, chorizo . . . |
| Carmen: | **Una ración de calamares** y una de aceitunas, por favor. |
| Camarero: | En seguida, señores. |

### Ordering drinks

| | |
|---|---|
| **¿Qué van a tomar, señores?** | What will you have? |
| **¿Quieren algo para comer?** | Do you want anything to eat? |
| **Hay anchoas, aceitunas, chorizo, calamares fritos . . .** | We have anchovies, olives, garlic sausage, fried squid. . . |
| **En seguida. . .** | At once. . . |
| **¿Qué tomas?** | What'll you have? |
| **Una coca-cola, por favor.** | A coke, please. |
| **Para mí un vermut** | For me a vermouth |
| **. . . con hielo y limón** | . . . with ice and lemon |
| **Quiero un zumo de naranja.** | I want orange juice. |
| **Yo quiero un vaso de vino tinto.** | I'd like a glass of red wine. |
| **Una cerveza, por favor.** | A beer, please. |
| **¿Qué tapas hay?** | What appetizers do you have? |

### Las bebidas (drinks)

| | |
|---|---|
| **el vino tinto/ blanco/rosado** | red/white/rosé/ wine |
| **seco/dulce** | dry/sweet |
| **el jerez fino/amon- tillado/oloroso** | dry/medium dry sweet sherry |
| **la cerveza** | lager, beer |
| **. . . de barril** | draft beer |
| **la sangría** | wine punch |
| **el ginebra** | gin |
| **el vermut** | vermouth |
| **el cuba libre** | rum and coke |

### Los refrescos (soft drinks)

| | |
|---|---|
| **el café, café solo** | black coffee |
| **café con leche** | coffee with milk |
| **la leche** | milk |
| **el agua** | water |
| **el té** | tea |
| **té con leche** | tea with milk |
| **el chocolate** | chocolate |
| **un batido** | milkshake |
| **una naranjada** | orangeade |
| **una limonada** | lemonade |
| **una gaseosa** | fizzy drink |

## How to ask

| | | | |
|---|---|---|---|
| Un tinto, por favor. | A red wine, please. | Un vaso de . . . | A glass of . . . |
| Una botella de . . . | A bottle of . . . | Un zumo de . . . | A . . . juice |
| Que esté bien frío | Nice and cold | . . . naranja/limón. . . | . . . orange/lemon |
| Con hielo | With ice | Un taza de . . . | A cup of . . . |
| con gas/sin gas | carbonated/noncarbonated | una coca-cola | coke |

## Las tapas (appetizers)

(Use **una ración de** when asking for a portion.)

| | | | |
|---|---|---|---|
| salchichón | sausage | jamón serrano | cured ham |
| queso | cheese | gambas | prawns, shrimp |
| champiñones | mushrooms | mejillones | mussels |
| aceitunas | olives | anchoas | anchovies |
| cacahuetes | peanuts | almejas | clams |
| patatas fritas | potato chips | calamares | squid |
| tortilla española | Spanish omelette | pulpo | octopus |
| chorizo | spiced and seasoned pork sausage | sepia | cuttlefish |

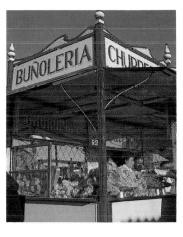

## Snacks

Although **tapas** can be very substantial, if you want something even more filling you can buy many different kinds of carryout food. Street vendors sell **helados** (ice cream) and **churros** (long, thin sticks of fried batter dipped in sugar).

## Los bocadillos (sandwiches made with French-type bread)

| | |
|---|---|
| un bocadillo de queso/de jamón | a cheese/ham sandwich |
| de calamar/de tortilla | a squid/omelette sandwich |
| ¿Qué bocadillos hay? | What sandwiches are there? |
| Uno de queso, por favor. | A cheese sandwich, please. |

## Other snacks

| | | | |
|---|---|---|---|
| un sándwich (caliente) | toasted sandwich | ¿Es para tomar ahora? | Is it to eat now? |
| una hamburguesa | hamburger | Para llevar | To go |
| un helado de vainilla/de fresa | | a vanilla/strawberry ice cream | |
| de chocolate/de pistacho | | a chocolate/pistachio ice cream | |

## the way it works

### People and things

The word for "a" is **un** for masculine words and **una** for feminine words: e.g., **un** vaso (a glass), **una** casa (a house).

In the plural **un** becomes **unos** and **una** becomes **unas**: e.g., un**os** calamar**es** (some squid), un**as** aceitun**as** (some olives).

### There is, there are

Note the following expressions from the dialogue:
**Hay** dos cuartos de dormir. There are two bedrooms.
**Hay** una vista maravillosa. . . There is a wonderful view. . .
**Hay** is used in both singular and plural, and is the same in question form:
¿Qué tapas **hay**?　　What tapas are there?

### Describing people and places

Adjectives such as modern**o** ( = modern), maravillos**a** ( = wonderful), bonit**o** ( = pretty) have **-o** and **-a** endings which change according to the gender of the word they accompany:

un**a** cocina modern**a**; un**a** vist**a** maravillos**a** (feminine)
**un** cuart**o** bonit**o**; **un** cuart**o** modern**o** (masculine)
un**a** casa vie**ja** (an old house)
**un** jardín pequeño (a small garden)

Some adjectives, however, including grand**e** ( = big) and amabl**e** ( = kind), do not change in the singular. *Note:* adjectives usually follow the noun.

With a plural word most adjectives add an **-s**: e.g., un**os** cuart**os** bonit**os**.

### Going places

¿Cuándo **vamos**?　　When do we go?
**Vamos** el miércoles.　　We are going on Wednesday.

**Vamos** is part of the verb **ir** (to go). Here is the present tense:

| | | | |
|---|---|---|---|
| **voy** | I go, am going | **vamos** | we go, are going |
| **vas** | you go, are going | **vais** | you go, are going |
| **va** | he/she/it goes, is going | **van** | they go, are going |
| | you go (formal) | | you go (formal) |

### Saying what you want

One of the first things you need to say is "I want." You can do this simply by stating the object and adding "please": **Una coca-cola, por favor.** Or say:

**Quiero** una coca-cola. (from **querer**, to want)　I want a Coca-Cola.
**Queremos** unas tapas.　　　　　　　　We want some tapas.

The complete pattern of the present tense of **querer** is as follows:

| | | | |
|---|---|---|---|
| **quiero** | I want | **queremos** | we want |
| **quieres** | you want | **queréis** | you want |
| **quiere** | he/she wants | **quieren** | they want |
| | you want (formal) | | you want (formal) |

## things to do

**4** **¿Cómo es tu casa?** Can you describe your own house or apartment? Use
some of the words on page 10: **moderno/viejo/bonito/grande/pequeño**.

1 ¿La casa? Es grande.      4 ¿El cuarto de baño?
2 ¿El cuarto de estar?      5 ¿El jardín?
3 ¿La cocina?      6 ¿Tu cuarto de dormir? (or . . . dormitorio?)

**5** You are in a café with a group of people. The waiter asks you what you
want: **¿Qué quieren ustedes?**
You are the only person who can speak Spanish, so you do the talking . . .

Ann:      [coffee with milk] Un café con leche, por favor.
Thomas:      [a red wine]
Alice:      [a cup of tea with lemon]
Isabel:      [a beer]
Martin:

Now choose what you want yourself:
Y yo quiero . . .

**6** It is time for a snack. First you go to a café-bar to buy a sandwich:
Camarero:      ¿Qué va a tomar, señor/a?
You:      [Ask what sandwiches there are]
Camarero:      Hay de jamón, queso, chorizo, calamares . . .
You:      [Say you'd like a ham sandwich, please]
Camarero:      En seguida, señor/a.

Next you spot an ice cream stand . . .

You:      [Ask what ice cream there is]
Ice cream vendor:      Tengo vainilla, fresa, chocolate, limón, pistacho . . .
You:      [Say you want a strawberry one, please]

**7** Can you sort out which question goes with which answer?

1 ¿Qué tomas?      **(a)** Está en el garaje.
2 ¿Cómo se llama la madre?      **(b)** El domingo.
3 ¿Cómo es la casa?      **(c)** Una cerveza, por favor.
4 ¿Dónde está el coche?      **(d)** Es muy moderna.
5 ¿Cuándo vamos a la playa?      **(e)** Se llama Caterina.

## TALKING ABOUT ONESELF

## ¿de dónde es?/where are you from?

While Carmen is at work, Tom is arranging to rent a car for Thursday, and the manager is filling out a form and asking him some questions.

Gerente: Usted no es español, ¿verdad?
Tom: **No, no soy español, soy inglés.**
Gerente: Habla muy bien el español, señor.
Tom: Muchas gracias. **Pues mi esposa es española. Es de Santander.**
Gerente: ¿Es usted de Londres?
Tom: No, no soy de Londres. **Vivo en Southampton** pero **trabajo en Londres.**
Gerente: ¿En qué trabaja?
Tom: **Soy director de una empresa de computadoras.**
Gerente: ¿Está aquí de negocios?
Tom: No, yo estoy de vacaciones pero mi esposa está de negocios. **Es periodista.**
Gerente: ¿Y su dirección aquí en Madrid, por favor?
Tom: Es la calle del Duque de Sesto 72, tercer piso.
Gerente: Muy bien. **Tiene su permiso de conducir, ¿verdad?**
Tom: Sí. **Aquí tiene usted.**

## Nationality and language

| | |
|---|---|
| ¿Es usted español/española? | Are you Spanish? |
| No, soy inglés/inglesa. | No, I'm English. |
| Soy alemán/americano. | I'm German/American. |
| Son canadienses/escocesas. | They are Canadian/Scottish. |
| Mi esposa es española. | My wife is Spanish. |
| Mi marido es español. | My husband is Spanish. |
| Hablo inglés. | I speak English. |
| ¿Habla usted francés? | Do you speak French? |
| No hablo español. | I don't speak Spanish. |
| Hablo un poco de alemán. | I speak a little German. |
| Entiendo/No entiendo . . . | I understand/I don't understand. . . |
| Habla muy bien el español. | You speak Spanish very well. |
| Hable más despacio, por favor. | Speak more slowly, please. |

## Where are you from?

| | |
|---|---|
| ¿Es usted de Londres? | Are you from London? |
| Es de Santander. | She is from Santander. |
| Soy de Boston. | I am from Boston. |
| ¿De dónde eres/es? | Where are you from? |
| ¿Dónde vive usted? Vivo en . . . | Where do you live? I live in . . . |
| Su dirección, por favor. | Your address, please. |

## What do you do? *(See also list on p. 80.)*

| | |
|---|---|
| ¿En qué trabaja usted? | What is your job? |
| ¿En qué trabajas? | What do you do for a living? |
| Soy director. | I am a director. |
| una empresa de computadoras | a computer firm |
| Trabajo en . . . | I work in . . . |
| ¿Está aquí de negocios? | Are you here on business? |
| Estoy de vacaciones. | I am on vacation. |
| Es periodista | She is a journalist. |

*Note:* to say "I am a teacher," etc., in Spanish you say: **Soy profesor**, etc., without using the indefinite article.

## Documents

| | |
|---|---|
| Su pasaporte, por favor. | Your passport, please. |
| ¿Tiene su permiso de conducir? | Do you have your driver's license? |
| Aquí tiene usted. | Here you are. |

## How old are you?

| | |
|---|---|
| ¿Cuántos años tiene/tienes? | How old is he/are you? |
| Tiene dos años. | He is two. |
| Tengo cuarenta y cinco años. | I'm 45. |

## Marital status

**Soy casado/casada.**  I am married.  **Soy soltero/soltera.**  I am single.

## *the way it works*

### Talking about yourself

When talking about yourself, your nationality, where you are from, what your profession is, etc., you always use the verb **ser**.

| | |
|---|---|
| **Soy** inglés. | I am English. |
| **Somos** de Manhattan. | We are from Manhattan. |
| **Es** estudiante. | He is a student. |

### Verb groups

Note these expressions from the dialogues:

| | |
|---|---|
| **Habla** muy bien el español. | You speak Spanish very well. |
| **Trabajo** en Londres. | I work in London. |

These examples come from a group of regular Spanish verbs, the **-ar** group, so called because all the infinitives (or dictionary forms) end in **-ar**. The present tense of these verbs is as follows:

habl**ar**, *to speak*

| | | | |
|---|---|---|---|
| habl-**o** | I speak | habl-**amos** | we speak |
| habl-**as** | you speak | habl-**áis** | you speak |
| habl-**a** | he/she speaks | habl-**an** | they speak |
| | you speak (formal) | | you speak (formal) |

There are two other verb groups, the **-er** group and the **-ir** group. Here is a regular example of the **-er** group:

beb**er**, *to drink*

| | | | |
|---|---|---|---|
| beb-**o** | I drink | beb-**emos** | we drink |
| beb-**es** | you drink | beb-**éis** | you drink |
| beb-**e** | he/she drinks | beb-**en** | they drink |
| | you drink (formal) | | you drink (formal) |

and one of the **-ir** group:

viv**ir**, *to live*

| | | | |
|---|---|---|---|
| viv-**o** | I live | viv-**imos** | we live |
| viv-**es** | you live | viv-**ís** | you live |
| viv-**e** | he/she lives | viv-**en** | they live |
| | you live (formal) | | you live (formal) |

### Do you have . . . ? (¿Tiene . . . ?)

| | |
|---|---|
| **¿Tiene** su permiso de conducir? | Do you have your driver's license? |
| Aquí **tiene** usted. | Here you are. (literally "you have it") |

These phrases contain examples of the verb **tener** (to have), which is used very frequently. It conveys the idea of *possession* and *availability*. It is also used when talking about *age*:

| | |
|---|---|
| ¿Cuántos años **tienes**? | How old are you? (literally, "How many years do you have?") |
| **Tengo** 23 años. | I'm 23. |

We will also meet **tener** + **que**, when it means "to have to":

| | |
|---|---|
| **Tengo que** ir al dentista. | I have to go to the dentist. |

Here is the complete pattern of the present tense of **tener**:

| | | | |
|---|---|---|---|
| **tengo** | I have | **tenemos** | we have |
| **tienes** | you have | **tenéis** | you have |
| **tiene** | he/she/it has | **tienen** | they have |
| | you have (formal) | | you have (formal) |

## things to do

**1**  **¿En qué trabajas?** (What do you do?) Can you sort out what everyone does by linking them with their place of work?

| | | | | |
|---|---|---|---|---|
| **1** Soy | secretaria | Trabajo en | **(a)** | un hospital |
| **2** | profesor | | **(b)** | una fábrica (factory) |
| **3** | enfermera | | **(c)** | una tienda (shop) |
| **4** | mecánico | | **(d)** | una oficina |
| **5** | ingeniero | | **(e)** | un taller (garage) |
| **6** | dependienta | | **(f)** | un colegio |

**2**  You do it too! (Use **también** = too, also)
Example: Carmen habla español. Yo también hablo español.

**1** Luisa habla inglés.
**2** Juan estudia idiomas.
   (studies languages)
**3** Tom trabaja en Londres.

**4** Carmen y Tom hablan español.
Nosotros también . . .
**5** Miguel y Luisa estudian español.
Nosotros también . . .

**3**  Can you describe your friend? Here are some useful words: **amable** (kind), **alto** (tall), **grande** (big), **bajo** (short), **simpático** (nice), **gordo** (fat), **guapa** (pretty).

You are asked to describe your Spanish friends to someone who wants to meet them. Here is the description of Miguel:

"Se llama Miguel. Miguel es inglés. Es de Londres. Habla español e inglés. Tiene 14 años. Es alto y delgado ( = *slim*). Tiene una hermana que se llama Luisa."

**1** Eduardo (from Madrid—accountant, aged 24—short and fat—one brother)
**2** Can you describe yourself? *(See p. 80 for list of jobs.)*
   Me llamo . . . (your name)          Soy de . . . (where you are from)
   Vivo en . . . (where you live)       Soy . . . (what you do)
   Trabajo en . . . (where you work)    Tengo . . . (your age)

**4**  Everyone is telling you where they live.

**1** Yo . . . en Madrid. ¿Dónde . . . usted?
**2** Yo . . . en Tarragona, pero mi hermano . . . en Valencia.
**3** Nosotros . . . en Toledo. Y vosotros, ¿dónde . . . ?
**4** Y ellos, ¿dónde . . . ? ¿En Salamanca? No, . . . en Ciudad Real.

## PUBLIC TRANSPORTATION

## ¿qué hora es?/what's the time?

Juan and Luisa are having lunch together. Juan has a sudden thought. . .

| | |
|---|---|
| Juan: | **¿Qué hora es, por favor?** |
| Luisa: | Pues, **son las tres y media** . . . |
| Juan: | ¡Hombre!**¿Son ya las tres y media?** ¡Me voy ahora mismo! Tengo una cita con el dentista a las cuatro y cuarto. **Adiós, hasta luego.** |
| Luisa: | **Hasta luego.** |

### Telling the time

| | |
|---|---|
| **¿Qué hora es, por favor?** | What time is it, please? |
| **¿Son ya las tres y media?** | Three-thirty already? |
| **Me voy ahora mismo.** | I must go/leave right now. |
| **Tengo una cita con el dentista** | I have a dentist appointment |
| **a las cuatro y cuarto** | at a quarter after four |
| **antes/después** | before/after |

### Saying goodbye

| | | | |
|---|---|---|---|
| **Adiós.** | Goodbye. | **Hasta la vista.** | Till we meet again. |
| **Hasta luego.** | See you later. | **Hasta mañana.** | Till tomorrow. |

**Spanish trains** The Spanish National Rail Network is called **RENFE** (**Red Nacional de los Ferrocarriles Españoles**). There are many different kinds of trains, and variations in fares, so it is necessary to be specific when asking for information. Here is a list of the main trains:

| | |
|---|---|
| el tranvía/ómnibus | slow train; makes every stop |
| el rápido | fast train; makes several stops |
| el expreso | long-distance night train; rather slow |
| el TALGO/TER | high-speed intercity express train |

You pay a supplement to travel on many fast or long-distance trains. The cheapest days to travel are Blue Days (**Días Azules**) when, for long journeys, you can normally get a 20% reduction on individual round trip tickets. There are also other discounts available for families, groups, senior citizens, etc. Tickets bought in advance include a seat reservation, and you will therefore be asked what train you wish to take. Advance reservations are recommended, especially for intercity trains.

## ¿ a qué hora hay tren?/when is there a train?

When Juan returns he telephones the RENFE office (**la oficina de viajes RENFE**) to find out the times of the trains to Santander the next day.

| | |
|---|---|
| Empleada: | Dígame. |
| Juan: | Buenos días. **¿A qué hora hay trenes para Santander,** por favor? |
| Empleada: | ¿Cuándo quiere viajar? |
| Juan: | **Mañana por la mañana.** |
| Empleada: | **El Talgo sale a las ocho veinticinco** y hay un rápido a las once treinta. |
| Juan: | **¿A qué hora llega el Talgo a Santander?** |
| Empleada: | A las catorce cuarenta y cinco. |
| Juan: | **¿Hay que reservar asientos en el Talgo?** |
| Empleada: | Sí, señor. |
| Juan: | Gracias, señorita. |
| Empleada: | De nada. Adiós. |

## en el despacho de billetes/in the ticket office

The three go to the Chamartín Station to buy tickets for the next day.

| | |
|---|---|
| Empleada: | ¿Qué desean ustedes? |
| Juan: | **Tres billetes de segunda clase para Santander,** por favor. |
| Empleada: | Sí, señor. ¿De ida o de ida y vuelta? |
| Juan: | **De ida y vuelta.** |
| Empleada: | ¿Para qué tren? |
| Juan: | **Para mañana, para el Talgo** de las ocho veinticinco. |
| Empleada: | Muy bien. Aquí tienen sus billetes. |
| Juan: | Gracias. **¿Cuánto es, por favor?** |
| Empleada: | Son doce mil treinta pesetas. |
| Juan: | Hay restaurante en el tren, ¿verdad? |
| Empleada: | Sí, señor. |

### Station notices

| | |
|---|---|
| **Estación de ferrocarril** | Railway station |
| **Trenes de cercanías** | Local/suburban trains |
| **Trenes de largo recorrido** | Long-distance trains |
| **Despacho de billetes** | Ticket office |
| **Llegadas/Salidas** | Arrivals/Departures |
| **Sala de espera/Consigna** | Waiting room/Baggage claim |
| **Horario/Destino** | Timetable/Destination |

### Train information

| | |
|---|---|
| **la agencia de viajes** | travel agency |
| **la taquilla** | ticket window |
| **Venta anticipada** | Sale of tickets in advance |
| **¿A qué hora hay trenes para . . .?** | At what time are there trains for . . .? |
| **¿A qué hora sale . . .?** | What time does . . . leave? |
| **¿A qué hora es el próximo tren para . . .?** | What time is the next train to . . .? |
| **¿Cuándo quiere viajar?** | When do you want to travel? |
| **Mañana por la mañana** | Tomorrow morning |
| **El Talgo sale a . . .** | The Talgo leaves at . . . |
| **¿A qué hora llega . . .?** | What time does it arrive? |
| **¿Hay que reservar asientos?** | Do you have to reserve seats? |
| **¿Hay que pagar suplemento?** | Do you have to pay a surcharge? |
| **¿Hay restaurante/coche-cama?** | Is there a dining car/sleeping car? |
| **¿Hay coche-literas?** | Are there berths? |
| **¿De qué andén sale?** | Which platform does it leave from? |
| **Vía número tres** | Platform three |
| **¿Lleva retraso?** | Is it late? |
| **¿Cuánto tiempo tarda?** | How long does it take? |
| **fumador/no fumador** | smoker/nonsmoker |

**Traveling by bus and coach**   City buses are usually pay-as-you-enter and are run on a flat fare system. Before getting on the bus, check which number and route you want on the bus-stop sign. In Madrid, as well as the normal buses of the state-run **EMT (Empresa Municipal de Transportes)**, there are also privately run minibuses which are more expensive.

Intercity buses link Madrid with the provincial capitals and some villages and towns. Bus fares are fixed by the length of the journey, and on some long-distance routes, tickets are obtainable in advance.

## *Bus information*
### (see also train section above)

| | |
|---|---|
| ¿A qué hora hay autobús/autocar para . . .? | What time is there a local/intercity bus to . . .? |
| es el próximo autobús? | is the next bus? |
| es el último autobús? | is the last bus? |
| Hay uno a . . . | There's one at . . . |
| ¿De dónde sale? | Where does it leave from? |
| Parada/Estación de autobuses | bus stop/station |
| plazas libres | seats free (available) |
| completo | full bus |
| Entrega de equipajes | Baggage check in |
| Recogida de equipajes | Baggage claim (pick-up) |

## *Buying a ticket*

| | |
|---|---|
| un billete | a ticket |
| Tres billetes para Santander | Three tickets to Santander |
| de segunda clase/de primera clase | second/first class |
| de ida/de ida y vuelta | one way/round trip |
| ¿Para qué tren? | For which train? |
| No quedan billetes. | There are no tickets left. |
| Aquí tienen sus billetes. | Here are your tickets. |
| ¿Cuánto es? | How much is it? |
| una reserva de asiento | a seat reservation |
| ¿Hay reducciones para niños? | Are there discounts for children? |
| Sólo para menores de 12 años | Only for children under 12 |
| ¿Hay reducciones para estudiantes? | Are there student discounts? |
| una tarjeta familiar | a family ticket |
| un billete entero | one full-price ticket |
| un billete de niño | one child's ticket |

**Plan of the Madrid Underground (Metro)**

Line 1
Line 2
Line 3
Line 4
Line 5
Line 6
Line 7
Ramal
Suburbano
under construction

## Listen for the following phrases

| | |
|---|---|
| Vía número cuatro | Platform/Track number four |
| El tren con destino a . . . | The train for . . . |
| El tren procedente de . . . | The train from . . . |

▶▶▶ **Traveling by metro** There are good subway or metro systems in
Madrid and Barcelona, open from 5 am to 11 pm. Fares are inexpensive
and are organized on a flat-fare basis. When you buy a ticket, check
which line you want (**Línea**) and the name of the last station on the line
(**Dirección**). To make a connection, look for the sign that says
**Correspondencias**.

## Metro (subway) travel

| | |
|---|---|
| Uno, por favor. | One, please. |
| ¿Qué línea es para . . .? | What line is for . . .? |
| La dos | Number two |
| ¿Tengo que hacer transbordo? | Do I have to transfer? |
| No, es directo. | No, it's direct. |
| Sí, en Goya | Yes, at Goya station |
| Línea/Dirección | Line/direction |
| Correspondencia | Connection |
| Devuelve cambio | Change given |
| Precio exacto | Exact change/fare |

**SALIDA**

**BILLETES**

## Air travel information

| | |
|---|---|
| ¿A qué hora hay vuelos a Sevilla? | At what time are there flights to Seville? |
| ¿Hay un vuelo a Londres hoy? | Is there a flight to London today? |
| Hay uno a las once de la mañana. | There's one at eleven in the morning. |
| Quisiera reservar un asiento. | I'd like to reserve a seat. |
| ¿Es un vuelo directo? | Is it a direct flight? |
| ¿Dónde está el terminal aéreo? | Where is the air terminal? |

**Taxis**   Fares vary in different areas, but taxi drivers should have a list of approved fares for local runs. There is a basic initial charge, and additional surcharges will be added to the meter at night, on weekends, and on holidays.

## Other notices

| | |
|---|---|
| Parada de autobuses | Bus stop |
| Estación de autobuses | Bus station |
| Parada de taxis | Taxi stand |
| Oficina de Información | Information Office |
| Vuelos internacionales | International flights |
| Vuelos nacionales | Domestic flights |
| Salida | Exit |

## Asking and telling the time/¿Qué hora es?

To ask the time in Spanish use the verb **ser**: **¿Qué hora es?** What time is it?

The answer is either **Es la una** (*It's one o'clock*) or **Son las dos, tres,** etc. (*it's two, three o'clock*). (For numbers, see p. 79.)

| | | | |
|---|---|---|---|
| Son las dos y cinco | It's 2:05 | Son las tres menos cinco | It's 2:55 |
| Son las dos y diez | It's 2:10 | Son las tres menos diez | It's 2:50 |
| Son las dos y cuarto | It's 2:15 | Son las tres menos cuarto | It's 2:45 |
| Son las dos y veinte | It's 2:20 | Son las tres menos veinte | It's 2:40 |
| Son las dos y veinticinco | It's 2:25 | Son las tres menos veinticinco | It's 2:35 |
| Son las dos y media | It's 2:30 | | |

To say "am" and "pm" you say:

Son las diez **de la mañana**. It's 10:00 am.        A las cinco **de la tarde**. At 5 pm.
Son las diez **de la noche**. It's 10:00 pm.

## 24-hour clock

Official time in Spain is calculated on the 24-hour clock. So for train, bus, and air schedules, opening and closing times, etc., be prepared to hear, for example, the phrases on the following page.

El vuelo número IB367 con destino a Neuva York sale a las quince veinte.
El expreso sale de Madrid a las dieciocho veinte y llega a Murcia a las seis de la mañana.

Note that the 24-hour clock leaves out **y** and **menos**: quince veinte = 15:20; quince cincuenta = 15:50.

### *How to say "to" and "from," etc.*

**De** is used to mean "of" or "from":

| | |
|---|---|
| Sale **de** Madrid | It leaves *from* Madrid |
| las ocho **de** la mañana | 8 o'clock *in (of)* the morning |
| **de** segunda clase | second class |
| la maleta **de** Luisa | Luisa's suitcase (suitcase *of* Luisa) |

**A** means "at" or "to":

| | |
|---|---|
| ¿**A** qué hora? | *At* what time? |
| Voy **a** Santander | I'm going *to* Santander |
| Llega **a** Santander | It arrives *at* Santander |
| **a** las diecinueve cuarenta | *at* 19:40 |

Another useful word in this dialogue is **para**, which means "for."

| | |
|---|---|
| los trenes **para** Santander | the trains *for* Santander (para = destination) |
| **para** dos personas | *for* two people |
| **para** hoy/**para** mañana | *for* today/*for* tomorrow BUT |
| **por** la mañana | *in* the morning (por = *during*) |

### *It leaves at ten*

**Sale** a las ocho veinticinco.    It leaves at 8:25. (from **salir**)
**Llega** a las catorce.    It arrives at 14:00. (from **llegar**)

You will find both these verbs are very useful. While **llegar** is a regular -**ar** verb (like **trabajar**), **salir** is an -**ir** verb with an irregular first person form:

| | | | |
|---|---|---|---|
| **salgo** | I leave | **salimos** | we leave |
| **sales** | you leave | **salís** | you leave |
| **sale** | he/she/it leaves | **salen** | they leave |
| | you leave (formal) | | you leave (formal) |

## things to do

**2.5**    **¿Qué hora es?** You are with a group of people and someone stops you to ask the time. The trouble is that everyone's watch says something different! **Son las . . .**

**6** ¿A qué hora hay autobús para Segovia?

| Destino | Salida | Destino | Salida |
|---------|--------|---------|--------|
| Segovia | 10:15 | Badajoz | 5:45 |
| Ávila | 15:30 | Huelva | 9:30 |
| Valladolid | 10:35 | Toledo | 11:25 |

Can you say what time the buses run:
¿A qué hora hay autobús para Segovia?　Hay uno a las diez y cuarto.

1 ¿A qué hora hay autobús para Toledo?
2 ¿A qué hora hay autobús para Ávila?
3 ¿A qué hora hay autobús para Badajoz?
4 ¿A qué hora hay autobús para Huelva?
5 ¿A qué hora hay autobús para Valladolid?

**7** Look at the price information sheet and answer:

| | Ida | Ida y vuelta |
|---|---|---|
| Madrid-Santander | 3.700 ptas | 5.000 ptas |
| Madrid-Barcelona | 4.200 ptas | 7.500 ptas |
| Madrid-Torremolinos | 4.500 ptas | 6.200 ptas |

1 Quiero un billete de ida para Santander. ¿Cuánto es? Son
2 Quiero un billete de ida y vuelta para Barcelona. ¿Cuánto es? Son . . .
3 Quiero un billete de ida para Torremolinos. ¿Cuánto es? Son . . .

**8** (a) You overhear the ticket agent advising a passenger about trains. Can you guess what the passenger is asking?

Passenger:　¿ . . . . . . . . . . . . . . . . . . . . . . . . . . . . . . . . . . . ?
Agent:　El próximo tren para Sevilla sale a las nueve doce.
Passenger:　¿ . . . . . . . . . . . . . . . . . . . . . . . . . . . . . . . . . . . ?
Agent:　Llega a las quince treinta.

(b) **En el metro.** Juan wants to go to Colón station for his dentist appointment. Can you fill in his part of the conversation?

Juan:　[One, please]
Agent:　Aquí tiene. Ciento ochenta pesetas.
Juan:　[Ask what line is for Colón]
Agent:　Es la cuatro.
Juan:　[Ask if you have to transfer]
Agent:　No, es directo.

# SHOPPING

▶ ▶ ▶ **Shopping**   Shops are usually open from 9:30 am to 1:30 pm and from 4 pm to 7:30 or 8:00 pm. As in America, department stores sell a wide range of goods, including furniture (**muebles**), records (**discos**), clothes (**ropa**), gifts (**regalos**), etc. Most credit cards (**tarjetas de crédito**) are accepted in most large shops, but it is best to check beforehand as they are not as widely used in Spain as in Britain and the United States.

## los grandes almacenes/the department store

Carmen wants to buy a leather jacket and she goes to the Nuevas Galerías (a big department store). There she talks to a sales clerk.

| | |
|---|---|
| Dependienta: | ¿Qué desea, señora? |
| Carmen: | **Quisiera una chaqueta de cuero.** |
| Dependienta: | ¿Es para usted? ¿Cuál es su talla? |
| Carmen: | **La cuarenta y dos.** |
| Dependienta: | (shows her some) ¿Le gusta este estilo? |
| | Tenemos en negro, marrón y azul oscuro. |
| Carmen: | Sí, **el estilo me gusta, pero no me gusta el color.** |
| | Me gusta más la negra—es más elegante. |
| | **¿Puedo probármela?** |
| Dependienta: | Sí, señora. Pase por aquí, por favor. |
| | (Carmen tries it on but finds it too small.) |

| | |
|---|---|
| Carmen: | ¡Qué lástima! No me sienta bien. **Es demasiado pequeña.** ¿Me puede enseñar otra más grande? |
| Dependienta: | Claro, señora, aquí está. (she tries it on) ¿Qué le parece? |
| Carmen: | Sí, me parece muy bien. **¿Cuánto cuesta, por favor?** |
| Dependienta: | Cuesta diez mil quinientas pesetas. |
| Carmen: | Bueno, **me la quedo.** |

*Shopping—clothes and accessories*

| | |
|---|---|
| ¿Qué desea, señora? | What do you want, ma'am? |
| ¿Es para usted? | Is it for you? |
| ¿Cuál es su talla? | What is your size? |
| ¿Qué número tiene? | What size do you wear? (shoes) |
| ¿Le gusta este estilo/color? | Do you like this style/color? |
| Tenemos en negro/en marrón/en azul | We have it in black/brown/blue |
| Los probadores están allí. | The fitting rooms are over there. |
| Pase por aquí, por favor. | Come this way, please. |
| ¿Algo más? | Anything else? |
| Lo siento. | I'm sorry. |
| Es el/la más barato/a que tenemos. | It is the cheapest one we have. |
| | |
| Sólo quiero mirar. | I'm just looking. |
| Quiero/Quisiera . . . | I want/I'd like . . . |
| una chaqueta de cuero | a leather jacket |
| (Mi talla) es la cuarenta y dos. | (My size) is a 42. |
| Mi número es . . . | My size is . . . (shoes) |
| Me gusta/no me gusta | I like it/I don't like it |
| el color/el estilo | the color/the style |
| ¿Tiene algo en rojo/verde? | Do you have anything in red/green? |
| Me gusta más . . . | I prefer . . . |
| la negra | the black one |
| Es más elegante. | It's more elegant. |
| Me gusta mucho. | I like it very much. |
| ¿Puedo probármelo/probármela? | Can I try it on? |
| Me sienta bien (no me sienta). | It fits me (doesn't fit me). |
| Es demasiado pequeño/a, grande, corto/a, largo/a, caro/a | It's too small, big, short, long, expensive |
| ¿Hay otro más grande?/más barato? | Is there a bigger one?/cheaper one? |
| ¿Me puede enseñar otro/a . . .? | Can you show me another . . .? |
| ¿Cuánto cuesta? | How much does it cost? |
| Me lo quedo/me la quedo. | I'll take it. |
| Lo/la compro. | I'll buy it. |

## USEFUL WORDS AND PHRASES

| | |
|---|---|
| ¿Qué le parece? | What do you think? |
| Me parece muy bien. | I think it's fine. |
| ¡Qué lástima! | What a pity! |
| OFERTA/REBAJAS | SALE/BARGAINS |

25

| Clothes sizes—women | | | | | | | | | |
|---|---|---|---|---|---|---|---|---|---|
| American | 4 | 6 | 8 | 10 | 12 | 14 | 16 | | |
| Spanish | 38 | 40 | 42 | 44 | 46 | 48 | 50 | | |

| Collar sizes—men (approximate) | | | | | | | | | |
|---|---|---|---|---|---|---|---|---|---|
| American | 14 | 14½ | 15 | 15½ | 16 | 16½ | 17 | | |
| Spanish | 36 | 37 | 38 | 39/40 | 41 | 42 | 43 | | |

| Shoe sizes | | | | | | | | | |
|---|---|---|---|---|---|---|---|---|---|
| American | 5 | 6 | 7 | 8 | 9 | 10 | 11 | 12 | 13 | 14 |
| Spanish | 35 | 36 | 37 | 38 | 39 | 40 | 41 | 42 | 43 | 44 |

## en el estanco/at the tobacconist's

In Spain you do not normally need to go to the post office to buy stamps—you can buy them in an **estanco** (a tobacco shop) which usually sells postcards and stamps as well as tobacco and cigarettes (**cigarrillos**), and sometimes newspapers as well. Tom is choosing some postcards, but he is unlucky with the stamps. . .

| | |
|---|---|
| Tom: | **Quiero estas cuatro postales, por favor.** |
| Dependiente: | Sí, señor. Las postales cuestan quince pesetas. |
| Tom: | Y, **¿tiene usted sellos?** Quiero cuatro para Inglaterra. |
| Dependiente: | No, señor. **Tiene que ir a Correos. ¿Algo más?** |
| Tom: | ¿Tiene periódicos ingleses? |
| Dependiente: | Me parece que tengo uno . . . Pero no lo veo. Lo siento, señor, no queda ninguno. Hay un quiosco en la esquina. |
| Tom: | Gracias, entonces, **eso es todo.** |

### Buying postcards and stamps

| | |
|---|---|
| **Quiero estas cuatro postales.** | I want these four postcards. |
| **¿Tiene usted sellos?** | Do you have stamps? |
| **Cuatro para los Estados Unidos.** | Four for the United States. |
| **Tiene que ir a Correos.** | You'll have to go to the post office. |
| **¿Algo más?** | Anything else? |
| **¿Tiene usted periódicos/revistas ingleses/-as?** | Do you have English newspapers/ magazines? |
| **Me parece que tengo uno.** | I think I have one. |
| **Pero no lo veo.** | But I don't see it. |

No me queda ninguno.
Hay un quiosco en la esquina.
Eso es todo.

I have none left.
There's a newsstand on the corner.
That's all.

## the way it works

### This and that

The word for "this" is **este** for masculine nouns and **esta** for feminine nouns:

**este** estilo     this style       **esta** chaqueta     this jacket

To say "that" you normally use **ese, esa**:

**ese** color     that color       **esa** camisa     that shirt

In the plural the pattern is as follows:

est**os**, est**as**     these       es**os**, es**as**     those

To say "this one" or "that one" use **éste, ésta** or **ése, ésa** with an accent. In a less specific sense **esto, eso** can also mean "this" and "that."

### More or less

The word for "more" is **más** and "less" is **menos**: **más grande** (bigger); **más pequeño** (smaller), **más caro** (more expensive); **más barato** (cheaper). To say "bigger than" or "more . . . than" you use **más . . . que**.

Este traje es **más grande que** el otro. (bigger than the other)
Esta camisa es **más cara que** la otra. (more expensive than the other)

If you want to say "biggest" or "the most . . ." you can use **el/la más**:

Esta camisa es **la más grande**. (the biggest)
Este vestido es **el más barato**. (the cheapest)

### Object pronouns

#### (1) Direct

¿El periódico? No **lo** veo.     The newspaper? I don't see it.
¿La chaqueta? **La** compro.     The jacket? I'll buy it.
¿Los zapatos? Me **los** quedo.     The shoes? I'll take them.
¿Las postales? No **las** veo.     The postcards? I don't see them.

As well as *it* and *them* we sometimes use a person as the object, e.g., *me* or *you*:

**La** conozco/**las** conozco     I know her/them (fem.)
**Le** veo/**les** veo     I see him/them (masc.)
**Me** ve/**te** ve     He sees me/he sees you

Here is a list of direct object pronouns:

| | | | |
|---|---|---|---|
| **me** | me | **nos** | us |
| **te** | you | **os** | you |
| **le/la** | him, her | **les/las** | them (people) |
| | you (masc./fem.) | | you (masc./fem.) |
| **lo/la** | it (masc./fem.) | **los/las** | them (things) |

**(2) Indirect**

| | |
|---|---|
| ¿**Me** puede enseñar otro? | Can you show *(to) me* another one? |
| ¿Qué **le** parece? | How does it seem *to you*? |

Here is a list of indirect object pronouns:

| | | | |
|---|---|---|---|
| **me** | to me | **nos** | to us |
| **te** | to you | **os** | to you |
| **le** | to him/her | **les** | to them (people) |
| | to you | | to you |
| **le** | to it | **les** | to them (things) |

Note that the object pronoun normally comes *before* the verb. When the verb is in the infinitive, however, the object pronoun may either precede or follow, in which case it is added on to the infinitive itself: ¿Puedo **probármela**? (Can I try it on?).

## *How to say "I like it"*

Look at the following phrases taken from the dialogues:

| | |
|---|---|
| ¿Le gusta este estilo? | Do you like this style? |
| Sí, me gusta. | Yes, I like it. |
| No me gusta el color. | I don't like the color. |
| Me gusta más . . . | I prefer . . . |
| Me gusta mucho. | I like it very much. |

From these examples you can see that the word "like" is used in a different way from English. **Me gusta el estilo** (I like the style) really means "the style is pleasing to me" (indirect object). With more than one thing use gust**an**.

| | |
|---|---|
| Me gustan estas camisas. | I like these shirts. |

Here is the verb in full:

| | | | |
|---|---|---|---|
| **me gusta(n)** | I like | **nos gusta(n)** | we like |
| **te gusta(n)** | you like | **os gusta(n)** | you like |
| **le gusta(n)** | he/she likes | **les gusta(n)** | they like |
| **le gusta(n)** | you like (formal) | **les gusta(n)** | you like (formal) |

## *things to do*

**3.1** Carmen is describing to her sister some of the clothes she has seen. For colors and materials, see p. 80.

**1** Q. ¿El vestido (*dress*) es rojo y negro?
   A. Sí, es rojo y negro.

**2** Q. ¿La falda (*skirt*) es verde?

**3** Q. ¿La camisa (*shirt*) es amarilla?
      Y, ¿es de seda o de algodón?

**4** Q. ¿ El suéter es marrón?
      Y, ¿es de lana o de acrílico?

**5** Q. ¿Los pantalones son grises?

**2** You are in a department store buying a tee-shirt (**una camiseta**). Can you fill in your part of the conversation?

Clerk:      ¿Qué desea, señorita?
You:        [Say you want a tee-shirt]
Clerk:      ¿Qué talla tiene?
You:        [Say you take a 44]
Clerk.      ¿Le gusta ésta?
You:        [Say you like the style but not the color]
Clerk:      La tenemos también en rojo y en azul.
You:        [Say you prefer the blue. Ask if you can try it on]
Clerk:      ¿Qué le parece, señorita?
You:        [Say you like it and ask how much it is]
Clerk:      Cuesta mil ochocientas cuarenta pesetas.
You:        [Say you'll buy it]

**3** See how difficult it is to get a good fit!

Clerk:      ¿Le gusta este traje?
You:        No, es demasiado . . . ¿Hay otro más . . .?
Clerk:      ¿Le gusta esta camisa?
You:        . . . . . . . . . . . . . . . . . . . . . . . . . . . . . . . .
Clerk:      ¿Le gusta este sombrero?
You:        . . . . . . . . . . . . . . . . . . . . . . . . . . . . . . . .
Clerk:      ¿Le gustan estos vaqueros?
You:        Son . . . . . . . . . . . ¿Hay otros más . . .?
Clerk:      ¿Le gustan estos zapatos?
You:        . . . . . . . . . . . . . . . . . . . . . . . . . . . . . . . .

**4** ¿**Cuánto cuesta?** Can you say the prices of these articles in Spanish?

**5** **Tienes que ir a la librería.** Can you match the following items with the shops where you can buy them? (See p. 81 for a list of shops.)

| | |
|---|---|
| **1** una pila (battery) | **(a)** la ferretería |
| **2** un diccionario (dictionary) | **(b)** el quiosco |
| **3** un perfume | **(c)** la tienda de aparatos eléctricos |
| **4** un periódico (newspaper) | **(d)** la perfumería |
| **5** un sacacorchos (corkscrew) | **(e)** la papelería |
| **6** un mapa (map) | **(f)** la librería |

# BUYING FOOD

▶▶▶ **Food shops**   There are several names for a grocery store in Spain—
**tienda de comestibles, alimentación, tienda de ultramarinos.** You
can, of course, also buy food in the market (**mercado**) and supermarket
(**supermercado**), and there are also increasing numbers of hypermarkets
(**hipermercados**), oversized stores for food, clothing, and a wide variety of
goods.

## en la tienda de comestibles/at the grocery store

Juan, Luisa, and Miguel have arrived in Santander and are stocking up on
groceries.

| | |
|---|---|
| Luisa: | Mantequilla, leche, galletas, anchoas y frutas. |
| Dependiente: | Buenos días, señorita. ¿Qué desea? |
| Luisa: | **Deme doscientos gramos de jamón . . ., medio kilo de** salchichas . . ., **cien gramos de** chorizo . . ., medio kilo de este queso manchego . . ., cien gramos de mantequilla . . ., y **un litro de** leche, por favor. |
| Dependiente: | ¿Algo más, señorita? |
| Luisa: | Sí. **Póngame un paquete de** esas galletas, y una lata de anchoas . . ., y **un kilo de** manzanas . . . Y ya está. |
| Miguel: | Oye, Luisa, mira estos melocotones. Me gustan muchísimo los melocotones y están bien maduros. ¿Qué te parece? |

| Luisa: | Bueno, chico, **vamos a comprar medio kilo de** melocotones para ti. Y eso es todo. ¿Cuánto es, por favor? |
| Dependiente: | Son novecientas sesenta y cinco pesetas en total, señorita. |
| Luisa: | Vale. (hands him the money) ¿Tiene una bolsa de plástico, por favor? |
| Dependiente: | Aquí tiene. Adiós, señorita. |

## *Shopping—food*

| | |
|---|---|
| **¿Qué tenemos que comprar?** | What do we have to buy? |
| **Deme doscientos gramos de . . .** | Give me 200 grams of . . . |
| **este queso manchego** | this cheese from La Mancha |
| **. . . medio kilo de jamón** | . . . half a kilo of ham |
| **. . . cuarto de kilo de salchichón/ salchichas** | . . . quarter of a kilo of (large) sausage/sausages |
| **. . . cien gramos de mantequilla** | . . . 100 grams of butter |
| **. . . un litro de leche** | . . . 1 liter of milk |
| **¿Algo más?** | Anything else? |
| **Póngame un paquete de . . .** | Give me a packet (package) of . . . |
| **esas galletas** | those crackers (cookies) |
| **. . . una lata de anchoas** | . . . a can of anchovies |
| **. . . un kilo de manzanas** | . . . a kilo of apples |
| **una rodaja de . . .** | a slice of . . . |
| **un trozo de . . .** | a piece of . . . |
| **Y ya está.** | And that's it. |
| **estos melocotones** | these peaches |
| **Me gusta(n) muchísimo . . .** | I adore . . . |
| **Está(n) bien maduro(s).** | It is/They are nice and ripe. |
| **¿Qué te parece?** | What do you think? |
| **Vamos a comprar . . .** | We'll buy . . . |
| **¿Cuánto es, por favor?** | How much is it, please? |
| **Son novecientas sesenta y cinco ptas** | That's 965 pesetas |
| **Vale** | O.K. |
| **¿Tiene una bolsa de plástico?** | Do you have a plastic bag? |
| **Aquí tiene.** | Here you are. |
| **Congelados** | Frozen food |
| **un poco más/menos** | a little more/less |
| **bastante/demasiado** | enough/too much |

# GOING TO THE BANK

**Banks and currency exhanges**  Banking hours are from 9 am to 2 pm on Monday to Friday and from 9 am to 1 pm on Saturday. You can change money in some shops and hotels (look for the **Cambio** sign) as well as in banks, but you will get a better rate of exchange in a bank. The basic unit of currency is the **peseta** and there are bills (**billetes**) in denominations of 100, 200, 500, 1,000, 2,000 and 5,000 pesetas, and coins (**monedas**) of 1, 5 (**un duro**), 10, 25, 50 and 100 pesetas.

## en el banco/in the bank

*En el banco/at the bank*

Tom goes to the bank to cash some traveler's checks:

| | |
|---|---|
| Tom: | Buenos días. **Quisiera cambiar unos cheques de viajero, por favor.** |
| Empleada: | Sí, señor. ¿Cuánto quiere cambiar? |
| Tom: | Cien libras. **¿A cómo está el cambio hoy?** |
| Empleada: | A ciento noventa y seis pesetas. ¿Su pasaporte, por favor? . . . Firme usted aquí. . . . ¿Quiere pasar a la caja, por favor? |
| Cajero: | ¿Cómo quiere su dinero, señor? |
| Tom: | Pues, **deme tres billetes de cinco mil pesetas** y el resto en billetes de menor valor. |

*Money language*

| | |
|---|---|
| Cambio | Exchange |
| Quisiera cambiar . . . | I'd like to change . . . |
| unos cheques de viaje/ viajero | some traveler's checks |
| unas libras esterlinas | some pounds sterling |
| unos dólares | some dollars |
| ¿Cuánto quiere cambiar? | How much do you want to change? |
| Cien dólares | $100 |
| ¿A cómo está el cambio? | What is the exchange rate? |
| A ciento noventa y seis | 196 pesetas |
| Firme usted aquí. | Sign here. |
| ¿Quiere pasar a la caja? | Please go to the cashier. |
| ¿Cómo quiere su dinero? | How do you want your money? |
| Deme tres billetes. | Give me three bills. |
| el resto | the rest |
| menor valor | lesser value |
| ¿Puede darme cambio? | Can you give me change? |
| las monedas | coins |
| los eurocheques | Eurocheques |
| la tarjeta de crédito | credit card |
| la carta de crédito | letter of credit |
| Quiero abrir una cuenta | I want to open an account |
| acreditar esto | to credit this |

## the way it works

*Asking how much*

There are several ways to ask the price of things. Here Luisa uses:

| | |
|---|---|
| **¿Cuánto es?** | How much is it? |

You will also hear:

**¿Cuánto cuesta/n?**   How much is it/are they?
**¿Cuánto vale/valen?**   How much is it/are they (worth)?

In the bank Tom asks the exchange rate:

**¿A cómo está el cambio?**   What is the exchange rate?

### We'll buy half a kilo/Vamos a comprar medio kilo.

The useful phrase **voy a . . . + infinitive** is the simplest way of expressing the future tense:

**Vamos a** tomar una copa.   We'll have a drink.
**Voy a** ver.   I'll go and see.
¿Qué **van a** tomar?   What will you have (to eat/drink)?

## things to do

**6**   Your friend has a long shopping list. Can you tell him where to go for each item? (See also list on p. 81.)

**1** el pan          (a)  la pastelería
**2** la carne        (b)  la tienda de comestibles
**3** las naranjas    (c)  la pescadería
**4** la leche        (d)  la frutería
**5** el azúcar       (e)  la panadería
**6** el pescado      (f)  la tienda de vinos
**7** el vino         (g)  la lechería
**8** un pastel       (h)  la carnicería

**.7**   This is your shopping list. Can you ask for each item in turn? (for numbers see p. 79)

250g butter
1 litre milk
500g ham
1 packet biscuits
1 tin sardines
1 kilo bananas
½ kilo peaches
6 pears
1 litre oil
2 bottles red wine
12 eggs

Start by saying: Quiero . . . Deme . . . Póngame . . .

**3.8** How much does it all cost? **¿Cuánto es todo?**

Work out how much the following will cost you per item, and then give the total: **un paquete de café; una docena de huevos; medio kilo de plátanos; dos kilos de tomates.**

**3.9** You are in a **tienda de comestibles** buying various items.

| | |
|---|---|
| Shopkeeper: | Hola, buenos días. |
| You: | [Say you want 200 grams of cheese and 100 grams of ham] |
| Shopkeeper: | ¿Y algo más? |
| You: | [Ask for half a kilo of apples and 6 ripe bananas] |
| Shopkeeper: | Muy bien. ¿Algo más? |
| You: | [Ask for a liter of milk. Say that's all and ask how much] |

**3.10** You are in a bank and you want to change some money.

| | |
|---|---|
| You: | [Say good morning. You want to change some dollars] |
| Clerk: | ¿Cuánto quiere cambiar? |
| You: | [$150. Ask what the exchange rate is] |
| Clerk: | A noventa pesetas. Firme aquí, por favor, y pase a la caja. |
| Cashier: | ¿Cómo quiere su dinero? |
| You: | [Say you want two 5,000 peseta bills, three 1,000 bills, and one 500 bill] |

**3.11** You are in a **pastelería** and your mouth is watering! (See list on p. 82.)

| | |
|---|---|
| Señora: | ¿Puedo ayudarle? |
| You: | [Say you'd like two of those cakes and a tart] |
| Señora: | ¿Algo más? |
| You: | [Say yes, ask her to give you a doughnut and bread roll] |
| Señora: | ¿Es para tomar ahora? |
| You: | [No, it's to go] |

## FINDING YOUR WAY

**La Oficina de Turismo** Most Spanish towns have a tourist office, which is usually the best place to obtain local maps and information about the region.

## ¿cómo puedo llegar a .../how do I get to ...?

Luisa and Miguel are trying to find their way around in Santander.

Luisa: **¿Dónde está la Oficina de Turismo, por favor?**

Passerby: **No está lejos. Van a pie, ¿verdad?**

Luisa: Si está cerca, vamos a pie.

Passerby: Pues, **tomen la primera calle a la derecha** y **sigan todo derecho.** Al final de esa calle llegan ustedes a la plaza. Está en la plaza **a la izquierda** enfrente de la Catedral.

Luisa: Gracias, señor. **¿Y hay un banco por aquí, por favor?**

Passerby: Sí, señorita. Hay muchos bancos. **Cojan la segunda calle a la derecha.** Hay un banco en la esquina al lado de la biblioteca.

| Miguel: | ¿No **se puede coger un autobús?** |
| Luisa: | ¡Qué perezoso eres! No, vamos andando. El banco está a unos diez minutos, nada más. Gracias, señor. |
| Passerby: | De nada, adiós. |

Tom is driving to Ávila with Carmen. He is not
quite sure of the way out of Madrid.

| Tom: | **Perdón, ¿la carretera de Ávila, por favor?** |
| Policeman: | Pues, siga hasta el final de esta calle y doble a la derecha. Tome la segunda calle a la izquierda y allí está la carretera. Se llama la Calle de la Princesa. |
| Tom: | Gracias. |

## *Asking the way*

| | |
|---|---|
| ¿Dónde está la Oficina de Turismo? | Where is the tourist office? |
| No está lejos. | It's not far away. |
| ¿Van a pie? | Are you going on foot? |
| Si está cerca. | If it's near. |
| Tome(n) la primera calle | Take the first street |
| a la derecha/a la izquierda | on the right/on the left |
| siga(n) todo derecho/recto | continue straight ahead |
| llegan ustedes | you'll arrive |
| a la plaza | in the square |
| enfrente de la Catedral | opposite the Cathedral |
| ¿Hay un banco por aquí? | Is there a bank near here? |
| Hay muchos bancos. | There are many banks. |
| Coja la segunda calle | Take the second street |
| en la esquina | on the corner |
| al lado de la biblioteca | beside the library |
| ¿No se puede coger un autobús? | Can't one take a bus? |
| Hay que coger un autobús. | You must take a bus. |
| Vamos andando/en coche/en autobús/ en taxi/en bicicleta/en motocicleta | We'll go on foot/by car/by bus/ by taxi/bike/motorcycle |
| Está a unos diez minutos. | It's about ten minutes (walk). |
| ¿La carretera de Ávila? | The road to Ávila? |
| Siga hasta el final de esta avenida | Go to the end of this avenue |
| Doble a la derecha | Turn right |
| ¿Cómo puedo llegar a . . .? | How can I get to . . .? |
| la parada está allí enfrente | The bus stop is opposite |
| Cambie de autobús | Change buses |

## OTHER USEFUL PHRASES

| | |
|---|---|
| ¡Qué perezoso eres! | What a lazybones you are! |
| Perdón | Excuse me |
| ¿Tiene un mapa de la ciudad? | Do you have a map of the city? |

**OFICINA
DE
TURISMO**

## the way it works

### Asking for directions

There are several ways to ask for directions.

| | |
|---|---|
| ¿La Catedral, **por favor?** | The Cathedral, *please?* |
| ¿**Dónde está** la estación? | *Where is* the station? |
| ¿**Por dónde se va a** la playa? | *How do you get to* the beach? |
| ¿**Cómo puedo llegar al** albergue de juventud? | *How can I get to the youth hostel?* |
| ¿**Para ir a** la playa? | *To get to* the beach? |
| ¿**Hay** un banco **por aquí?** | *Is there* a bank *near here*? |

### Understanding instructions

Not only might you have to ask the way, but you will also have to be able to understand the various ways in which instructions are given in Spanish. Look at the following phrases:

**Tomen** la primera calle . . . **sigan** todo derecho　　**Coja** la segunda calle . . .
**Doble** a la derecha . . . **Tome** el número dos . . . **Cambie** de autobús

These forms of the verbs are known as the imperative (or command). The imperative is formed by taking the stem of the first person ("I" form) of the present tense (e.g., **tom**-o, **coj**-o, **sig**-o) and adding the following sets of endings:

For -**ar** verbs, e.g., **tomar** (to take) add -e (sing.), -en (pl.): **tome, tomen; doble, doblen.**

For -**er** and -**ir** verbs, e.g., **seguir** (to follow), **subir** (to go up) add -**a** (sing.), -**an** (pl.): **siga, sigan; suba, suban.**

*Note:* the verb **ir** (to go) is irregular, the imperative being **vaya** (sing.) and **vayan** (pl.).

### Methods of transportation

Note the different ways of getting around: Vamos **a pie, en tren, en coche, en avión,** etc.

The verb **coger** is used for "to catch" or "take": "To get on (a bus)" is **subir** and "to get off" is **bajar: Subes** a la estación y **bajas** a la playa (You get on at the station and get off at the beach).

### Place and distance words

The following expressions are essential for giving directions and it is worth listening for them:

| | | | |
|---|---|---|---|
| **a la derecha** | to/on the right | **al lado (de)** | beside, next to |
| **a la izquierda** | to/on the left | **en la esquina** | on the corner |
| **todo derecho** | straight ahead | **al final (de)** | at the end (of) |
| **cerca (de)** | near (to) | **allí** | there |
| **lejos (de)** | far (from) | **aquí** | here |
| **aquí mismo** | right here | **enfrente (de)** | opposite, in front (of) |
| **hacia** | towards | **hasta** | until, up to |
| **por** | along | **por aquí** | hereabouts, around here |
| **detrás (de)** | behind | **delante (de)** | in front (of) |
| **al otro lado** | on the other side | | |

Notice the use of **primero, segundo,** etc.

**la primera** calle a la derecha     the first street on the right
**la segunda** calle a la izquierda    the second street on the left

Also, you may be told how long it will take to get to your destination:

Está **a unos quince minutos.**     It's about fifteen minutes away.
Está **a una hora de viaje** de aquí.   It's an hour's journey from here.

and the distance:

Está **a doscientos metros.**     It's 200 meters away.
Está **a cien kilómetros.**        It's 100 kilometers away.

## Poder (to be able) and volver (to return)

Some Spanish verbs change not only their endings but also the middle of the word.
In the case of both these **-er** verbs there is a vowel change from **o** to **ue** in the stem
of the 1st, 2nd and 3rd persons singular and 3rd plural.

| | | | |
|---|---|---|---|
| pue**do** | I can | pod**emos** | we can |
| pue**des** | you can (fam.) | pod**éis** | you can (fam.) |
| pue**de** | he/she/you can | pue**den** | they/you can |
| vue**lvo** | I return | volv**emos** | we return |
| vue**lves** | you return (fam.) | volv**éis** | you return (fam.) |
| vue**lve** | he/she returns, you return | vue**lven** | they/you return |

## Impersonal se

To say "Can one do this?" or "How do you get to . . .?" Spanish uses an impersonal
pronoun **se** which is the equivalent of *one, you, they,* etc. before the third person of
the verb:

¿Por dónde **se va** a la playa?       How does one get to the beach?
¿**Se puede** aparcar aquí?          Can you park here?
¿Dónde **se puede** comprar el pan?   Where can one buy bread?
¿No **se puede** coger un taxi?       Can't we take a taxi?

The answer is formed in exactly the same way, namely:

**Se va** por la plaza.             One goes through the square.
Sí, **se puede.**/No, **no se puede.**    Yes, you can./No, you can't.

## things to do

**4.1** Can you work out how to get there? Follow the example.
¿Por dónde se va a la catedral?    ➡ Tome la primera calle a la derecha.

**1** ¿ . . . a la iglesia? (church)

**2** ¿ . . . al museo? (museum)

**3** ¿ . . . al parque? (park)

**4** ¿ . . . a la plaza? (square)

2 You are in the Calle de Castilla, by the station. (☆ marks the spot.) Look at the map and find out where you are being directed to:

1 Tome la primera calle a la izquierda y luego la segunda a la derecha y siga todo derecho. Está a la izquierda.

2 Tome la tercera calle a la izquierda que se llama la Calle de la Lealtad y luego la primera a la derecha. Está allí en la plaza, enfrente de la Catedral.

3 Pase por delante de la Catedral hasta la Plaza Porticada. Esta alli a la izquierda.

4 Tome la primera calle a la derecha y en seguida doble a la derecha otra vez. Está a la derecha en la esquina.

5 Coja la primera calle a la izquierda y al final de esa calle tome la calle a la izquierda que se llama la Calle Alta. Siga todo derecho hasta el final y está allí a la izquierda.

| Key | (1) Aduana | (4) Plaza Porticada |
|---|---|---|
| | (2) Banco de España | (5) Oficina de Turismo |
| | (3) Catedral | (6) Ayuntamiento |

# DRIVING AND BREAKDOWNS

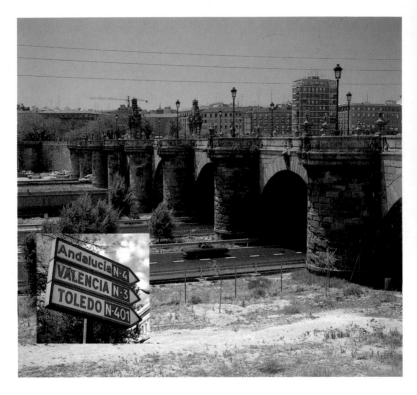

**Driving** An International Driver's License (or an authorized translation of your American license) is recommended, and you must have your license with you. It is compulsory to have your registration and adequate insurance. Spain adheres to the International Highway Code. Speed limits are normally:

| | |
|---|---|
| Freeways (**autopistas = A**) | 120 km/h (75 mph) |
| National Highways (**carreteras nacionales = N**) | 100 km/h (62 mph) |
| Other roads | 90 km/h (56 mph) |
| Residential areas | 60 km/h (37 mph) |

Gas stations are relatively infrequent outside the main towns, so it's advisable to fill up when you have an opportunity. There are two main grades of gas: **super** (97 octane) and **normal** (92 octane). You cannot always use your credit card. On most freeways a toll **(peaje)** is payable, the amount depending on the distance covered. Wearing a seatbelt **(cinturón de seguridad)** is compulsory.

## en la gasolinera/at the gas station

Tom and Carmen are in the car driving to Ávila. They stop to buy gas.

| | |
|---|---|
| Empleada: | Buenas tardes, señor. |
| Tom: | Buenas tardes. **Lleno de super, por favor.** |
| Empleada: | Bueno. Ya está, cuarenta y ocho litros. |
| Tom: | **¿Quiere comprobar el aceite y el agua,** por favor? |
| Empleada: | (Checks oil and water) Necesita medio litro de aceite. |
| Tom: | Muchas gracias. ¿Cuánto le debo? |
| Empleada: | Son cuatro mil trescientas pesetas. |

## el taller mecánico/the garage

Unfortunately, after setting off again, they have a flat tire and after changing the tire, they stop in at a garage on the outskirts of Ávila.

| | |
|---|---|
| Tom: | Hola, buenas tardes. Tengo un problema con el neumático. **¿Puede repararlo, por favor?** |
| Empleado: | Bueno, vamos a ver . . . Tiene un agujero bastante grande, pero creo que puedo hacerlo. ¿Puede volver dentro de un rato? |
| Tom: | Muy bien. Vuelvo en veinte minutos, ¿verdad? |
| Empleado: | Sí, señor. |

### Echando gasolina (putting in gas)

| | |
|---|---|
| **Lleno de super, por favor.** | Fill it up with super (premium), please |
| **Dos mil pesetas, por favor.** | 2,000 pesetas of gas, please. |
| **Cincuenta litros** | 50 liters |
| **la gasolina** | gas/gasoline |
| **el gasóleo** | diesel |
| **la gasolina sin plomo** | lead-free gasoline |
| **super/normal** | premium/regular |
| **¿Quiere comprobar . . . ?** | Please, could you check . . .? |
| **el aceite/el agua/la presión** | oil/water/tire pressure |
| **Necesita medio litro** | It needs half a liter |
| **¿Cuánto le debo?** | How much do I owe you? |

### Un pinchazo (a flat)

| | |
|---|---|
| **el taller** | garage, body shop |
| **¿Arregla usted pinchazos?** | Do you fix flat tires? |
| **¿Quiere reparar/arreglar . . .?** | Please repair/fix . . . |
| **¿Puede cambiar . . .?** | Can you change . . .? |
| **el neumático** | the tire |
| **Tiene un agujero.** | It has a hole. |
| **¿Puede volver dentro de un rato?** | Can you come back in a while? |

## Mi coche está averiado *(my car has broken down)*

(parts of the car are listed on p. 82)

| | |
|---|---|
| No funciona el motor | The engine is not working |
| Mi coche no quiere arrancar | My car won't start |
| ¿Dónde está el taller más cercano? | Where's the nearest garage? |
| ¿Puede mandar un mecánico? | Can you send a mechanic? |
| ¿Cuánto tiempo tardará? | How long will it take? |
| Puedo ponerlo en seguida | I can fit it at once |
| la marca/la matrícula | the make/the registration number |

### Road signs

| | |
|---|---|
| Ceda el paso | Give way, yield |
| ¡Cuidado! | Caution |
| Desviación | Detour |
| Dirección única | One-way street |
| Estacionamiento de automóviles | Parking |
| Estacionamiento prohibido | No parking |
| Obras | Roadwork (construction) |
| Paso prohibido | No entry |
| Peatones | Pedestrians |
| Peligro | Danger |
| Puesto de socorro | First aid station |

### After an accident

| | |
|---|---|
| Ha habido un accidente. | There has been an accident. |
| Hay gente herida. | Some people are hurt. |
| Llame la policía. | Call the police. |
| Llame una ambulancia/un médico. | Call an ambulance/a doctor. |
| ¿Cuál es su numbre/su dirección? | What is your name/address? |
| su permiso de conducir | your driver's license |
| sus papeles de seguro | your insurance papers |

### OTHER USEFUL PHRASES

| | |
|---|---|
| Ya está. | That's it. |
| Bueno, vamos a ver. | Well, let's have a look. |
| ¿Cuánto le debo? | How much do I owe you? |
| Tengo un problema con . . . | I have a problem with . . |

# ILLNESS AND INJURY

▶▶▶

**Illness**   In cases of minor injuries and illnesses, you may find the pharmacist very helpful. Pharmacists may sell and recommend medicine often only available by prescription in the U.S. If you take prescription medicine, always carry your prescription with you.

## me duele la cabeza/I have a headache

Pilar doesn't feel well and goes to the doctor.

Médico:  Hola, buenas tardes, siéntese por favor.
Pilar:   Buenas tardes, doctor.
Médico:  Vamos a ver, ¿qué le pasa?
Pilar:   **No me siento bien. Me duele la cabeza,** no tengo apetito y me parece que **tengo fiebre.**
Médico:  **¿Desde cuándo se siente así, señora?**
Pilar:   Desde hace unos días . . . Y **me siento mareada** cuando me levanto por la mañana.
Médico:  Por favor, **tiéndase aquí. Voy a hacerle un examen.** (Examines her) Por favor **abra la boca . . . Respire profundo.** . . . No se preocupe, señora, no es grave. **Tiene una gripe** y debe quedarse en cama. **Aquí tiene una receta** . . . Tome dos cucharadas cada tres horas. ¡Adiós, que se mejore pronto!
Pilar:   Gracias y adiós.

*En el consultorio (in the doctor's office)*

| | |
|---|---|
| Siéntese, por favor. | Sit down, please. |
| ¿Qué le pasa? | What's wrong? |
| No me siento bien. | I don't feel well. |
| Me duele la cabeza/ el estómago/la espalda | I have a headache/ a stomachache/a backache |
| No tengo apetito. | I have no appetite. |
| Tengo fiebre. | I have a temperature (fever). |
| Me siento mareada | I feel dizzy |
| cuando me levanto | when I get up |
| ¿Desde cuándo se siente así? | How long have you been feeling like this? |
| Desde hace unos días. | For a few days. |
| Tiéndase aquí. | Lie down here. |
| Voy a hacerle un examen. | I'm going to examine you. |
| Abra la boca. | Open your mouth. |
| Respire profundo. | Breathe deeply. |
| No se preocupe. | Don't worry. |
| No es grave. | It's not serious. |
| Tiene una gripe. | You have the flu. |
| Debe quedarse en cama. | You must stay in bed. |
| Aquí tiene una receta. | Here is a prescription. |
| Tome dos cucharadas | Take two tablespoonfuls |
| cada tres horas | every three hours |
| ¡Que se mejore pronto! | Get better soon! |

43

## Things the doctor should know

| | |
|---|---|
| Soy alérgico a . . . | I'm allergic to . . . |
| . . . la penicilina | . . . penicillin |
| Soy diabético. | I'm diabetic. |
| Tomo la píldora. | I'm on the pill. |
| Estoy embarazada. | I'm pregnant. |

## Things that can happen to you

(Parts of the body are listed on p. 82.)

| | |
|---|---|
| Me duele el . . ./la . . . | My . . . hurts |
| Me he roto . . ./Me he quemado . . . | I have broken . . ./I have burned . . |
| Me he torcido . . ./Me he cortado . . . | I have twisted . . ./I have cut . . . |
| Me ha picado un mosquito. | A mosquito has bitten me. |
| Tengo una insolación. | I have sunstroke. |
| Tengo diarrea | I have diarrhea |
|     resfriado/catarro |     a cold/flu |
|     anginas/tos |     a sore throat/cough |
|     un moretón/una ampolla |     a bruise/a blister |
|     una quemadura/un salpullido |     a burn/a rash |
|     una picadura (de insecto) |     a sting (insect)/bite |
|     una intoxicación/una indigestión |     food poisoning/indigestion |
| Tengo dolor de (estómago). | I have a (stomach) ache. |
| He tenido vómitos. | I've been vomiting. |
| Estoy estreñido. | I am constipated. |
| ¿Necesito una receta? | Do I need a prescription? |

▶ ▶ ▶ **Pharmacies**   These are identified by a green or red cross. Business hours are the same as other shops, but they are usually closed on Saturday afternoons. Each pharmacy remains open one night a week from 9 to 10 pm, and an emergency service is assured by a rotation system during holidays, at night and on weekends. Look for the on-duty sign **Farmacia de Guardia,** posted on pharmacy doors and printed in the local papers.

## en la farmacia/at the pharmacy

Luisa has hay fever and goes to a pharmacy in Santander.

| | |
|---|---|
| Luisa: | **¿Puede darme algo para la fiebre del heno, por favor?** |
| Druggist: | Sí señorita. (hands her a packet of pills) Tiene que tomar un comprimido cada cuatro horas. Son trescientas pesetas. |
| Luisa: | Muchas gracias, adiós. |

### At the pharmacy

(Pharmaceutical items and toiletries are listed on p. 81.)

| | |
|---|---|
| ¿Puede darme algo para . . .? | Can you give me something for . . .? |
| la fiebre del heno | hay fever |
| Tiene que tomar un comprimido/ la medicina | You must take a pill/tablet/ the medicine |
| cada cuatro horas/dos veces al día | every 4 hours/twice a day |

## the way it works

### Making polite requests

*Note:*

| | |
|---|---|
| ¿**Quiere** comprobar el aceite? | Would you please check the oil? |
| ¿**Quiere** arreglar el neumático | Would you please repair the tire? |
| ¿**Puede** volver dentro de un rato? | Could you come back in a while? |

### Reflexive verbs

| | | |
|---|---|---|
| No **me** siento bien. | I don't feel well | (sentirse = to feel) |
| . . . cuando **me** levanto | . . . when I get up | (levantarse = to get up) |

These are examples of verbs being used reflexively, indicating actions done by, to, or for oneself. The object of the verb is usually the same as the subject. Reflexive verbs are accompanied by a reflexive pronoun: **me** (myself), **te** (yourself), **se** (him/her/itself), **nos** (ourselves), **os** (yourselves), **se** (themselves):

| | | |
|---|---|---|
| **Me** llamo. . . | I am called . . . | from llamar**se** (to be called) |
| **Te** levantas | You get up | from levantar**se** (to get up) |
| **Se** abre | It opens | from abrir**se** (to open) |
| **Nos** bañamos | We bathe | from bañar**se** (to bathe) |
| **Se** sientan | They sit down | from sentar**se** (to sit down) |

Note that the reflexive pronoun comes before the verb unless that verb is in the infinitive or imperative:

Siénte**se**    Sit down! (sentarse)    *but*    No **se** preocupe.    Don't worry.

## I have a headache

Note that when talking about parts of your body you normally use "the" and not "a" or "my" as in English:

**Me** duele **la** cabeza.   I have a headache.
Abra **la** boca.   Open your mouth.

## How long ago . . .?

In Spanish use the phrase: **¿Desde cuándo?** + present tense.

¿Desde cuándo se siente así?   How long have you been feeling this way?

and the reply

**Desde hace** unos días   Since a few days ago
**Hace unos días**   A few days ago

**Hace** (it makes) is part of **hacer** (to do or to make). Here is the present tense:

| | | | |
|---|---|---|---|
| **hago** | I make | **hacemos** | we make |
| **haces** | you make | **hacéis** | you make |
| **hace** | he/she/it makes | **hace** | they make |
| | you make (formal) | | you make (formal) |

## things to do

**4.3**   You are at a gas station. Tell the attendant in Spanish:

**1** to fill up the tank   **3** to check the oil
**2** that you want 35 liters of premium   **4** to check the tire pressure

**4.4**   Your car has broken down and you are telephoning for help. You say:

**1** that your car won't start   **3** could they please send a mechanic?
**2** that the ignition isn't working   **4** how long will that take?

**4.5**   You are not feeling well. Can you describe your symptoms to the doctor?

Doctor:   Buenos días, ¿qué le pasa?
You:   [Say your stomach hurts and you have diarrhea]
Doctor:   ¿Desde cuándo se siente así?
You:   [For about a week]
Doctor:   Bueno, aquí tiene unos comprimidos para tomar tres veces al día.
You:   [Say thank you and goodbye]

**4.6**   In the pharmacy, you are looking for three items:

Phar.:   Buenos días, ¿puedo ayudarle?
You:   [Ask if she can give you something for insect bites]
Pharm.:   Aquí tiene. ¿Algo más?
You:   [Ask for some band-aids and some throat lozenges]

# HOTELS AND CAMPSITES

**Somewhere to stay**   There are five official categories of Spanish **hotels**, ranging from the luxurious 5-star downwards. A 3-star hotel will usually offer you your own bathroom. In addition to the top-class hotels, there are **paradores**, state-run hotels which are often built in beautiful locations and sometimes situated in converted palaces and castles.

Less expensive forms of accommodation include **hostales** (small, often family run, hotels) which are graded from 1 to 3 stars, **residencias** (economically priced hotels often without a restaurant), **pensiones** (boardinghouses often containing permanent residents), **albergues** (country inns), and **albergues de juventud** (youth hostels). The price of the room is written on a card on the back of the bedroom door, and does not vary according to the number of people in it. It does not always include breakfast. Prices of rooms throughout the range are generally cheaper than in the U.S. To book a hotel on the spot you can go to the local Tourist Office, but in the tourist season it is essential to make reservations in advance, particularly in the main tourist centers.

## *Looking for a hotel*

| | |
|---|---|
| **¿Dónde hay un hotel?** | Where is there a hotel? |
| **¿Hay un hotel cerca de aquí?** | Is there a hotel near here? |
| **Busco un buen hotel** | I'm looking for a good hotel |
| **en el centro de la ciudad** | in the center of the city (downtown) |

## ¿tiene una habitación doble?/do you have a double room?

As they are in the region of Ávila, Carmen and Tom decide to try their luck at a hotel recommended by Andrés Valbuena.

| | |
|---|---|
| Recepcionista: | Buenos días, señores. |
| Carmen: | Buenos días. **¿Tiene una habitación doble, por favor?** |
| Recepcionista: | ¿Para cuántas noches? |
| Carmen: | **Para dos noches.** |
| Recepcionista: | Bueno . . . ¿La quiere con baño, señora? |
| Carmen: | Sí, **con baño si es posible.** |
| Recepcionista: | Vamos a ver. (looks at list) Lo siento, señora. Tenemos habitaciones con lavabo pero no nos quedan con baño para hoy. |
| Carmen: | Bueno, no importa. **¿Cuánto es la habitación con lavabo?** |
| Recepcionista: | Son dos mil quinientas pesetas por noche. |
| Carmen: | **¿Está incluido el desayuno?** |
| Recepcionista: | Sí, todo incluido. |
| Carmen: | Está bien. |

### Reserving a room

| | |
|---|---|
| **Quisiera reservar una habitación** | I'd like to reserve a room |
| **para mañana/para miércoles** | for tomorrow/for Wednesday |
| **Lo siento. Está completo.** | I'm sorry, the hotel's full. |
| **¿Puede tener una habitación el jueves?** | Would you have a room on Thursday? |
| **He reservado una habitación.** | I have reserved a room. |
| **¿Hay habitaciones disponibles?** | Are there any rooms available? |
| **¿Tiene una habitación disponible?** | Do you have a room available? |
|   **para esta noche** | for tonight |
|   **para una noche** | for one night |
|   **para dos/tres noches** | for two/three nights |
|   **para una semana** | for a week |
|   **para el miércoles** | for Wednesday |
|   **para cuatro personas** | for four people |
| **Quiero una habitación doble** | I want a double room |
|   **individual/sencilla** | single |
|   **con baño/con ducha** | with a bathroom/a shower |
|   **con lavabo** | with a washbasin |
|   **con cama matrimonial/dos camas** | with a double bed/twin beds |
|   **con un balcón/vista al mar** | with a balcony/sea view |
| **Tenemos habitaciones con ducha** | We have rooms with a shower |
| **No nos quedan . . .** | We have no . . . left |
| **¿Cuál es el precio?** | What is the price? |
| **¿Cuánto es por día?** | How much is it per day? |
| **la pensión completa/la media pensión** | full board/half board |
| **Es demasiado caro.** | It is too expensive. |
| **¿Tiene algo más barato?** | Do you have anything cheaper? |
| **¿Está incluido el desayuno?** | Is breakfast included? |
| **planta baja** | ground floor |
| **primer/segundo/tercer piso** | first/second/third floor |

48

## he reservado una habitación/I have reserved a room

Andrés and his wife Asunción have reserved a room at the same hotel.

| | |
|---|---|
| Andrés: | Buenos días. **He reservado una habitación para dos noches.** |
| Recepcionista: | ¿Cuál es su nombre, por favor? |
| Andrés: | Andrés Valbuena. |
| Recepcionista: | Ah, sí, . . . una habitación doble con baño. ¿Quiere llenar esta ficha, señor, y me deja su pasaporte? |
| Andrés: | De acuerdo. (Fills in form) |
| Recepcionista: | Firme aquí, por favor . . . Gracias. Su habitación es el número quince en el segundo piso. Aquí tiene su llave. |
| Andrés: | Muchas gracias. **¿Se puede aparcar en la calle?** |
| Recepcionista: | No, en esta calle no se puede, pero hay un aparcamiento detrás del hotel. |

### At the hotel

| | |
|---|---|
| He reservado una habitación. | I have reserved a room. |
| **¿Cuál es su nombre?** | What is your name? |
| **¿Quiere llenar esta ficha?** | Please fill out this form. |
| Me deja su pasaporte | Let me have your passport |
| su carnet de identidad | your identity (I.D.) card |
| Es el número quince | It's number 15 |
| en el segundo piso. | on the second floor. |
| **Aquí tiene su llave.** | Here is your key. |
| **¿Puedo ver la habitación?** | Can I see the room? |
| **Esta habitación es demasiado pequeña.** | This room is too small. |
| **¿Me subirá el equipaje?** | Will you have the luggage taken up? |
| **¿Se puede aparcar en la calle?** | Can you park in the street? |
| **Hay un aparcamiento detrás del hotel.** | There's a parking lot behind the hotel. |

### While you are there . . .

| | |
|---|---|
| **Me da la llave, por favor.** | Please give me my key. |
| No funciona . . . | The . . . is not working |
| el agua caliente/fría | hot water/cold water |
| la luz/el interruptor de la luz | the light/the light switch |
| la radio/el televisor | the radio/the television set |
| **¿A qué hora es el desayuno?/** | What time is breakfast?/ |
| la comida?/la cena? | lunch?/dinner? |
| **¿Sirven el desayuno en la habitación?** | Do you serve breakfast in the room? |

*Paying the bill*

| | |
|---|---|
| ¿Me da la cuenta, por favor? | May I have the bill, please? |
| Creo que hay un error. | I think there is a mistake. |
| ¿Puedo pagar con cheque?/tarjeta de crédito? | May I pay by check?/credit card? |
| ¿Está incluido el servicio? | Is service included? |

**Camping**   If you want to camp, there are over 500 campsites to choose from, but it is advisable to reserve in advance for popular resorts in the high season. Camping I.D. cards are no longer required.

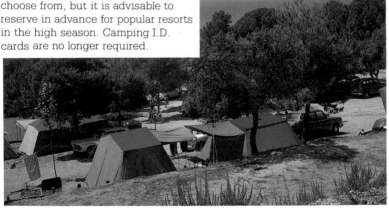

## ¿hay sitio?/is there a place?

Felipe, a student friend of Juan, has arrived with his tent at a campsite near Juan's house. He checks in at the office and talks to the guard.

| | |
|---|---|
| Felipe: | Buenas tardes, señor. **¿Hay sitio?** |
| Guardián: | Sí, hay varios sitios. ¿Cuántas personas son? |
| Felipe: | **Somos tres. Tengo un coche y una tienda.** |
| Guardián: | ¿Cuántas noches quieren pasar aquí? |
| Felipe: | **Dos noches, por favor.** |
| Guardián: | Puede ponerla allí. ¿Quiere llenar esta ficha, por favor? |
| Felipe: | De acuerdo. **¿Hay duchas calientes?** |
| Guardián: | Sí, pero no funciona el agua caliente en este momento. |
| Felipe: | Y, ¿hay electricidad? |
| Guardián: | Sí, ¿quieren toma de corriente? |
| Felipe: | Sí, por favor. |

| | |
|---|---|
| Prohibido acampar | No camping |
| ¿Hay sitio? | Is there a place? |
| Hay varios sitios. | There are various places. |
| ¿Cuántas personas son? | How many are you? |
| Somos dos. | We are two. (There are two of us.) |
| Tengo una tienda (de campaña) | I have a tent |
|     una caravana | a van |
| Puede ponerla allí. | You can put it over there. |
| ¿Quiere llenar esta ficha? | Please fill out this form. |
| ¿Se puede comprar gas butano? | Can you buy butane gas? |
| ¿Se puede alquilar un saco de dormir? | Can you rent a sleeping bag? |
| ¿Dónde están las duchas calientes?/ | Where are the hot showers?/ |
|    los cubos de basura? |    the trash cans? |
| ¿Dónde está el agua potable? | Where is the drinking water? |
| No funciona el agua. | The water isn't working. |
| los servicios/el retrete | toilets/lavatory |
| el agua/el grifo | water/tap |
| la piscina | swimming pool |
| ¿Hay electricidad? | Is there electricity? |
| ¿Quieren toma de corriente? | Do you want to plug in? |
| ¿Se puede encender una hoguera? | Can you make a bonfire? |

| | | | |
|---|---|---|---|
| **Teléfono** Telephone | **Acceso bus** Bus access | **Restaurante** Restaurant | **Piscina** Swimming pool | **Pesca superficie** Surface fishing |
| **Correos** Post Office | **Botella gas** Bottle gas | **Bar** Bar | **Duchas** Showers | **Equitación** Horse-riding |
| **Cambio moneda** Exchange | **Supermercado** Super market | **Cafetería** Cafeteria | **Playa** Beach | **Pista tenis** Tennis court |
| **Acceso autos** Car access | **Lavandería** Laundry facilities | **Enfermería** Sick bay (First aid) | **Pesca submarina** Underwater fishing | **Parque infantil** Children's playground |

## *the way it works*

### The Present Perfect Tense

**He reservado** una habitación.    I have reserved a room.

This is an example of the present perfect tense, which is used in very much the same way as in English. It is formed with a part of the auxiliary verb **haber** (to have) + a past participle:

| | | | |
|---|---|---|---|
| **he** reservado | I have reserved | **hemos** reservado | we have reserved |
| **has** reservado | you have reserved | **habéis** reservado | you have reserved |
| **ha** reservado | he/she has reserved | **han** reservado | they have reserved |
| | you have reserved | | you have reserved |

Note that the past participle **reservado** does not change its ending. Past participles are normally formed by taking the stem of the verb, e.g., **reserv-**, and adding on **-ado** (-ar verbs), or **-ido** (-er and -ir verbs).

## things to do

**5.1**  Practice reserving different rooms at a hotel.

Quiero una habitación . . .

**5.2**  You arrive at a hotel after having reserved a room. Can you fill in your part of the conversation with the receptionist?

You:      [Say good afternoon. You have reserved a room]
Recep.:   ¿Su nombre, por favor?
You:      [Give your name]
Recep.:   A ver . . . Sí. Una habitación sencilla, número doce. ¿Quiere firmar aquí, por favor? . . . ¿Tiene equipaje?
You:      [Say it's in the car]
Recep.:   El botones lo subirá. Aquí tiene su llave.
You:      [Thank you very much]

**5.3**  You want to reserve a room for the night but you left it to the last minute.

You:      [Ask if there is a room available]
Recep.:   Sí. ¿La quiere con baño?
You:      [No, say you want a room with a washbasin]
Recep.:   Sólo tenemos una doble con baño.
You:      [Ask how much the room is]
Recep.:   Tres mil seiscientas pesetas por noche.
You:      [Say you are sorry but it's too expensive]

**5.4**  You are making inquiries about a campsite.

You:        [Say good afternoon and ask if there is any room]
Guardián:   Sí, hay varios sitios. ¿Cuántas personas son?
You:        [Say you are four and that you have a van]
Guardián:   ¿Cuánto tiempo quieren quedarse?
You:        [A week]
Guardián:   Bueno. Pueden poner la caravana cerca de la playa.

**5.5**  You are checking up on the facilities of a certain campsite. ¿Hay . . .?

**5.6**  A lot of things don't seem to be working! Can you tell the guard?

**1** the hot showers   **2** the toilets   **3** the electricity   **4** the tap (faucet)   **5** the drinking water

# EATING OUT

**Restaurants and mealtimes** Spanish restaurants are officially classified by forks (**tenedores**); five forks is the most expensive, but you can often get a very good meal in a much more modest establishment. Look for the fixed price menu (**menú del día**) which usually offers three courses and is often a very good value. Cheaper restaurants will often serve a one-dish meal (**plato combinado**), which combines several courses on one plate. Service is usually included (**servicio incluido**), but many people will leave a little extra for really good service.

## en el restaurante/in the restaurant

Carmen and Tom have met up with Andrés and his wife Asunción and they have decided to eat out in a restaurant.

| | |
|---|---|
| Tom: | **¿Hay una mesa libre?** |
| Camarero: | ¿Es para cuántas personas, señor? |
| Tom: | **Somos cuatro.** |
| Camarero: | Pasen por aquí, señores. Tengo una mesa cerca de la ventana. |

(They sit down at the table)

| | |
|---|---|
| Camarero: | ¿Qué van a comer, señores? |
| Asunción: | **Vamos a tomar el menú del día. De primero** quiero el gazpacho andaluz y **de segundo** la chuleta de ternera. |
| Carmen: | **Pues, para mí** los espárragos y el lomo de cerdo. |
| Andrés: | **Yo voy a tomar** la sopa de pescado y el bistec a la parrilla. |
| Camarero: | ¿Cómo prefiere su bistec, señor? |
| Andrés: | **Lo prefiero poco hecho.** |
| Camarero: | (Turns to Tom) ¿Y usted, señor? |
| Tom: | **Pues a mí me gusta mucho** la paella. Voy a tomar la paella y una ensalada mixta. |
| Camarero: | Sí, señor. ¿Y para beber? |
| Tom: | **Tráiganos** una botella de Valdepeñas, y una botella de Chablis. |
| Carmen: | Y una botella de agua mineral, también. |
| Camarero: | En seguida, señores. |

(Later the waiter asks them what they want for dessert)

| | |
|---|---|
| Camarero: | ¿Qué quieren **de postre,** señores? |
| Carmen: | Un flan con nata, un helado de vainilla y una tarta de manzana. **Y la cuenta, también, por favor.** |

## Ordering a meal

*The table*

| | |
|---|---|
| ¿Puede recomendar un buen restaurante? | Can you recommend a good restaurant? |
| Quiero reservar una mesa para las nueve. | I want to make a reservation for nine o'clock. |
| ¿Hay una mesa libre? | Is there a table available? |
| ¿Para cuántas personas? | For how many? |
| Somos cuatro. | There are four of us. |
| Una mesa para seis, por favor. | A table for six, please. |
| Pasen por aquí. | Come this way. |
| cerca de la ventana | near the window |

*The menu*

| | |
|---|---|
| ¡Oiga! ¡Camarero! | Waiter! |
| Traiga el menú, por favor. | Bring the menu, please. |
| ¿Tiene un menú fijo? | Do you have a set menu? |
| Vamos a tomar . . . | We'll have . . . |
| el menú del día | the menu of the day |
| el menú gastronómico | the gourmet menu |
| ¿Qué recomienda hoy? | What do you recommend today? |
| ¿De qué consiste? | What does it consist of? |
| De primero/de segundo | For the first course/second course |
| gazpacho andaluz | cold tomato soup |
| chuleta de ternera | veal cutlet |
| puntas de espárragos | asparagus tips |
| lomo de cerdo | pork loin |
| sopa de pescado | fish soup |
| bistec a la parrilla | grilled steak |
| bien hecho, regular, poco hecho | well done, medium, rare |

| | |
|---|---|
| paella valenciana | saffron rice and seafood (mussels, shrimp, etc.), with pieces of chicken, peas and peppers |
| ensalada mixta | tossed salad |
| ¿Quiere algo de postre? | Would you like dessert? |
| No, gracias, no quiero nada. | No thank you, I don't want anything. |
| flan con nata | caramel custard with whipped cream |
| helado de vainilla | vanilla ice cream |
| tarta de manzana | apple tart |

*And to drink?*

| | |
|---|---|
| ¿Y para beber? | What do you want to drink? |
| la lista de vinos | the wine list |
| Una botella de . . . | A bottle of…(See also Unit 1 p. 9.) |
| ¿Tiene vino da la casa? | Do you have any house wine? |
| el agua mineral | mineral water |
| una coca-cola/una cerveza | a coke/a beer |
| café para todos | coffee for everyone |

*The check*

| | |
|---|---|
| La cuenta, por favor. | The check, please. |

**Meals**   Breakfast (**el desayuno**) is a light meal consisting usually of coffee and bread or sweetrolls. Lunch (**el almuerzo, la comida**) is the main meal of the day and is eaten much later than in the U.S., between 2 and 3 pm, followed by a siesta. However, the tradition of a long late lunch is changing in the cities, where you will often find it is eaten earlier; the siesta is tending to disappear. The evening meal (**la cena**) is also eaten later—at 9 or 10 pm.

## en el Hostal Lombraña/at the Hostal Lombraña

Juan meets his friend Felipe and together with Luisa and Miguel they go to a cheap restaurant in town. Juan is taking the orders.

| | |
|---|---|
| Juan: | Amigos, ¿qué vais a tomar? |
| Luisa: | **Para mí, de primero,** sopa de fideos, por favor. Y después una tortilla de jamón con ensalada. |
| Juan: | ¿Y tú, Miguel? |
| Miguel: | Pues, ¡yo tengo una hambre que me muero! **Voy a tomar** macarrones y albóndigas con salsa de tomate. |
| Juan: | Y ¿para ti, Felipe? |
| Felipe: | **Para mí un plato combinado.** Garbanzos y huevos con jamón. |
| Juan: | Y, ¿para beber? |
| Miguel: | Una coca-cola para mí, por favor. |
| Luisa: | Y para mí un zumo de naranja. |

| | |
|---|---|
| **Para mí** . . . | For me . . . |
| **sopa de fideos** | noodle soup |
| **tortilla de jamón con ensalada** | ham omelette and salad |
| **(No) tengo hambre.** | I am (not) hungry. |
| **¡Tengo un hambre que me muero!** | I am dying of hunger! |
| **Voy a tomar macarrones.** | I'll have macaroni. |
| **albóndigas con salsa de tomate** | meatballs in tomato sauce |
| **garbanzos** | chick-peas |
| **huevos con jamón** | ham and eggs |
| **(No) tengo sed.** | I am (not) thirsty. |

*Useful restaurant phrases*

| | |
|---|---|
| **pan y cubierto** | bread and cover charge |
| **menú turístico** | tourist menu |
| **menú del día** | menu of the day |
| **platos combinados** | combined dishes |
| **postre a elegir** | dessert choice |
| **servicio incluido** | service included |
| **sal y pimienta** | salt and pepper |
| **Señoras** | Ladies |
| **Caballeros** | Gentlemen |
| **la mesa** | table |
| **la silla** | chair |
| **el cuchillo** | knife |
| **el tenedor** | fork |
| **la cuchara** | spoon |
| **el plato** | plate, dish |
| **aceite y vinagre** | oil and vinegar |

❊❊❊ MENÚ DEL DÍA ❊❊❊

| | |
|---|---|
| *gazpacho andaluz* | *paella valenciana* |
| *sopa de pescado* | *huevos a la flamenca* |
| *puntas de espárragos* | *tortilla de jamón* |
| *ensalada mixta* | |

| | |
|---|---|
| *chuleta de ternera* | *flan con nata* |
| *lomo de cerdo* | *helado* |
| *bistec* | *tarta de manzana* |
| *conejo al limón* | *fruta del tiempo* |
| | *queso* |

## things to do

**5.7** Look at this menu and decide what you and your two friends would like to eat: **De primero . . ., de segundo . . ., de postre . . .**

**5.8** Things are not always easy when you try to order a meal . . .

| | |
|---|---|
| Waiter: | ¿Qué va a tomar, señor? |
| You: | [First, the mussels] |
| Waiter: | Lo siento, no tenemos hoy. |
| You: | [Well then, you'll have the fish soup] |
| Waiter: | Muy bien. ¿Y de segundo? |
| You: | [The codfish] |
| Waiter: | Lo siento, no queda . . . |
| You: | [Ask if he has fillet of sole] |
| Waiter: | Creo que sí, señor. ¿Y de postre? |
| You: | [An orange, please] |
| Waiter: | Sólo hay plátanos. |
| You: | [OK, you'll have a banana and could he bring the bill, please?] |

## SPORTS AND LEISURE

## ¿te gustan los deportes?/do you like sports?

Juan is talking to Miguel about sports.

Juan: **¿Qué deportes practicas** en Inglaterra?

Miguel: Pues, en invierno **juego al fútbol** y en verano al tenis. Pero soy muy malo para el tenis—**me gusta más** el fútbol.

Juan: **A mí me interesa la natación y la pesca,** sobre todo la pesca submarina.

Miguel: Y, **¿sabes hacer** esquí acuático?

Juan: Sí, **sé hacerlo pero prefiero la natación. Si te interesa** el fútbol, mañana hay un partido en el estadio. **¿Tienes ganas de** ir?

Miguel: ¡Oh sí! **Me gustaría mucho.** ¿Qué equipos juegan?

Juan: No sé, pero me parece que es un partido entre el Rácing y el Castellón.

Miguel: ¿A qué hora empieza?

Juan: **Empieza a las cinco de la tarde.** Bueno, hoy vamos a la taquilla para sacar las entradas.

| RESULTADOS CUATRO ÚLTIMAS TEMPORADAS | | | | | Al final del partido | | | | PRÓXIMO BOLETO |
|---|---|---|---|---|---|---|---|---|---|
| En el descanso | | | | Domingo 22 de noviembre | (6 de diciembre) | | | | |
| 83-84 | 84-85 | 85-86 | 86-87 | | 83-84 | 84-85 | 85-86 | 86-87 | |
| 1-0 | — | 1-0 | 2-0 | 1 Barcelona-Cádiz.......... | 4-1 | — | 1-0 | 2-0 | 1 Barcelona-Murcia |
| 0-0 | 0-0 | — | 1-0 | 2 Murcia-Betis .............. | 1-0 | 0-1 | — | 3-0 | 2 Betis-Real Sociedad |
| — | — | 1-0 | — | 3 Real Sociedad-Celta .. | — | — | 1-1 | — | 3 Celta-Valladolid |
| — | — | — | — | 4 Valladolid-Logroñés.... | — | — | — | — | 4 Logroñés-Real Madrid |
| 1-0 | — | — | 0-0 | 5 Real Madrid-Mallorca . | 2-0 | — | — | 3-0 | 5 Mallorca-Spórting |
| — | — | — | 1-0 | 6 Spórting-Sabadell ..... | — | — | — | 2-1 | 6 Sabadell-Zaragoza |
| 0-1 | 1-1 | 0-0 | 0-0 | 7 Zaragoza-At. Madrid .. | 2-2 | 1-1 | 0-0 | 1-0 | 7 At. Madrid-Osasuna |
| 1-0 | 0-2 | 0-0 | 0-0 | 8 Osasuna-Athlétic....... | 1-1 | 1-2 | 0-1 | 0-1 | 8 Athlétic-Las Palmas |
| 0-1 | 0-0 | 1-1 | 0-0 | 9 Sevilla-Español ......... | 2-1 | 0-0 | 1-1 | 1-0 | 9 Valencia-Sevilla |
| 0-1 | — | — | — | 10 Castellón-Rácing........ | 1-1 | — | — | — | 10 Cádiz-Español |
| — | — | 1-0 | 1-0 | 11 Sestao-Málaga .......... | — | — | 3-0 | 2-1 | 11 Rácing-Bilbao Ath. |
| 0-0 | — | 1-1 | 0-0 | 12 Recreativo-Elche ...... | 1-0 | — | 2-1 | 0-1 | 12 Burgos-Sestao |
| — | — | — | 0-0 | 13 Jerez-Oviedo ........... | — | — | — | 0-0 | 13 Málaga-Recreativo |
| 0-0 | 3-2 | 1-1 | 0-0 | 14 Deportivo-Cartagena . | 3-0 | 4-2 | 2-1 | 1-0 | 14 Oviedo-Hércules |

## An interest in sports

*(For a list of sports, see p. 83.)*

| | |
|---|---|
| ¿Qué deportes practicas? | What sports do you play? |
| en invierno/en verano | in winter/in summer |
| juego al fútbol, tenis | I play soccer, tennis |
| el fútbol americano | football |
| Soy muy malo para . . . | I'm very bad at . . . |
| Me gusta más el fútbol. | I like soccer better. |
| No me gusta nada. | I don't like it at all. |
| A mí me interesa la natación/ | I'm interested in swimming/ |
|    la pesca/la pesca submarina |    fishing/deep-sea fishing |
| ¿Sabes hacer el esquí acuático? | Do you know how to water-ski? |
| Sí, sé hacerlo. | Yes, I know how to. |
| Prefiero la natación. | I prefer swimming. |
| Si te interesa el fútbol | If you are interested in soccer |
| Hay un partido | There is a match (game) |
| en el estadio | in the stadium |
| ¿Tienes ganas de ir? | Would you like to go? |
| Me gustaría mucho. | I'd love to. |
| ¿Quiénes juegan? | Who is playing? |
| ¿A qué hora empieza? | What time does it begin? |
| Empieza a las . . . | It begins at . . . |
| Vamos a la taquilla . . . | Let's go to the ticket office . . . |
| . . . para sacar las entradas | . . . to buy the tickets |

## Buying tickets

| | |
|---|---|
| Dos entradas para el partido/ | Two tickets for tomorrow's game or |
|    la corrida de mañana |    match/bullfight |
| de tribuna/de general | in the grandstand/on the terrace |
| |    (general admission) |
| sol/sombra/sol y sombra | in the sun/shade/sun and shade |

# SIGHTSEEING

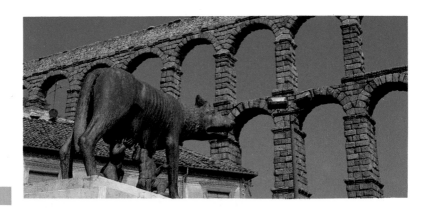

## haciendo turismo/seeing places

Tom and Carmen are in Segovia where they visit the Oficina de Turismo.

| | |
|---|---|
| Tom: | Buenas tardes. **Quisiera unos folletos sobre la región** y un plano de la ciudad, por favor. |
| Empleada: | Aquí tiene. ¿Algo más? |
| Tom: | **¿Tiene una lista de hoteles?** |
| Empleada: | Claro, señor. |
| Tom: | **¿Sabe a qué hora está abierto el Museo** del Alcázar? |
| Empleada: | Está abierto de nueve a doce y media por la mañana y de tres a siete por la tarde. |
| Tom: | Y, **¿cuánto vale la entrada?** |
| Empleada: | Trescientas cincuenta pesetas. |
| Tom: | Muchas gracias, señorita. |

| | |
|---|---|
| Quisiera unos folletos. | I'd like some brochures. |
| un plano de la ciudad | a map (plan) of the city |
| ¿Tiene una lista de hoteles? | Do you have a list of hotels? |
| ¿A qué hora está abierto . . .? | At what time is the . . . open? |
| ¿A qué hora se abre? | At what time does it open? |
| ¿A qué hora se cierra? | At what time does it close? |
| ¿Cuánto vale la entrada? | How much does a ticket cost? |
| entrada gratuita | free entrance |
| abierto/cerrado | open/closed |

### Places to see

| | | | |
|---|---|---|---|
| la catedral | cathedral | el museo | museum |
| el castillo, el alcázar | castle | el palacio | palace |
| la cueva | cave | el ayuntamiento | town hall |
| la iglesia | church | el parque | park |
| el claustro | cloister | la plaza de toros | bullring |
| la mezquita | mosque | el monasterio | monastery |

## the way it works

### More verbs with vowel changes

We have already seen some verbs which have a change of vowel in the present tense (see Jueves, por la mañana, p. 38). We have also seen the following very commonly used verbs:

| querer: | to want | } e→ie | quiero | I want |
|---|---|---|---|---|
| tener: | to have | | tienes | you have |

This stem change occurs usually in the 1st, 2nd and 3rd persons singular and the 3rd person plural. In this unit we have:

empezar    *to begin:*  empiezo, empiezas, empieza, empezamos, empezáis, empiezan

cerrar    *to close:*  cierro, cierras, cierra, cerramos, cerráis, cierran

We also have a verb with a different vowel change:

jugar    *to play* u → ue: juego, juegas, juega, jugamos, jugáis, juegan

## What do you know?

¿**Sabes** (hacer el esquí acuático)?    Do you know how to (water-ski)?
**Sé** . . .    I know how to . . .
No **sé**.    I don't know.

To know something, or to know how to do something in Spanish is **saber**.

| | | | |
|---|---|---|---|
| **sé** | I know | **sabemos** | we know |
| **sabes** | you know | **sabéis** | you know |
| **sabe** | he/she knows | **saben** | they know |
| | you know (formal) | | you know (formal) |

However, if you are talking about knowing a person or a place, you use the verb **conocer**.

No **conozco** la ciudad.    I don't know the city.
Encantado de **conocerle**.    Pleased to meet you.

Note that when talking about knowing a person, you insert **a** before that person.

**Conocen a** muchos americanos.    They know many Americans.

Here is the present tense:

| | | | |
|---|---|---|---|
| conozco | I know | conocemos | we know |
| conoces | you know | conocéis | you know |
| conoce | he/she knows | conocen | they know |
| | you know (formal) | | you know (formal) |

## Question words

Here is a list of some of the question words from the dialogues in this unit and elsewhere:

| | | |
|---|---|---|
| ¿**Qué**? | What? | ¿**Qué** deportes practicas? |
| ¿**Quién**?/¿**Quiénes**? | Who? | ¿**Quiénes** juegan? |
| ¿**Cuándo**? | When? | ¿**Cuándo** empieza? |
| ¿**Cuánto**? | How much? | ¿**Cuánto** vale la entrada? |
| ¿**Cuántos/as**? | How many? | ¿**Cuántas** personas son? |
| ¿**Cuál**? | Which? | ¿**Cuál** es su nombre? |
| ¿**Cómo**? | How? | ¿**Cómo** te llamas? (literally, How are you called?) |
| | | ¿**Cómo** es? (literally, How is it?) |

Note that question words always carry a written accent.

## *things to do*

**1**   You are being asked what sports you play.

| | |
|---|---|
| Interviewer: | ¿Qué deportes practicas? |
| You: | [Say you play tennis and you like swimming] |
| Interviewer: | ¿Te gusta también el fútbol? |
| You: | [Say you don't like it at all] |
| Interviewer: | ¿Sabes jugar al golf? |
| You: | [Yes, you know how to but you prefer tennis] |

**2**   ¿Te gusta el deporte? Me gusta.../No me gusta.../Soy muy malo para...

     **1** Luisa likes ball games but hates water sports. When asked what sports she likes, what does she say?

     **2** Juan likes most things to do with water, but is no good at ball games. When asked which sports he likes, what does he say?

     **3** Now can you say what sports or games you like, what you don't like, and what you are bad at?

**3**   Felipe takes Luisa to see the Tito Bustillo cave, where they talk to the **empleada**, the cashier.

| | |
|---|---|
| Felipe: | [Two tickets, please] |
| Empleada: | [Say how much two cost] |
| Felipe: | [Ask what time they open] |
| Empleada: | [Say they open at 3 pm] |

He also takes her to the Claustro Romano.

| | |
|---|---|
| Felipe: | [Two tickets, please] |
| Empleada: | [Say how much two cost] |
| Felipe: | [Ask what time it closes] |
| Empleada: | [Say it closes at 7 pm] |

**4**   Can you match the following questions and answers?

| | |
|---|---|
| 1 ¿Te gusta la equitación? | **(a)** Sí, sé hacerlo. |
| 2 ¿Qué equipo juega? | **(b)** Prefiero la pesca. |
| 3 ¿Prefieres la pesca o la natación? | **(c)** De nueve a doce. |
| 4 ¿Sabes jugar al ajedrez (chess)? | **(d)** No, no me gusta nada. |
| 5 ¿A qué hora está abierta? | **(e)** Juega el equipo de Salamanca. |

**5**   You are introduced to señor Santillana at a party (**una reunión**) and strike up a conversation with him. Can you ask these questions in Spanish?

     **1** Ask him if he knows Victor, a colleague from your office in Dallas.
        ¿Conoces a Víctor, un colega de mi oficina en Dallas?

     **2** Ask if he knows Conchita, a friend of your wife.

     **3** Does he know how to play chess?

     **4** Ask him if he knows when the party finishes, (una se termina)

     **5** Say you know your wife would like to meet him.

## VACATION PLANS

## las vacaciones/vacations

Carmen is interviewing various students about the sort of vacations they like.

Carmen: ¿Cuándo piensas ir de vacaciones este año?

Estudiante: Pues, **pienso ir a principios de septiembre.**

Carmen: Y, ¿adónde piensas ir? ¿Al extranjero, a las montañas, al mar?

Estudiante: Este **año voy a Cantabria**—primero a Santander.

Carmen: Y, ¿qué vas a hacer allí?

Estudiante: Voy a alquilar un coche y **visitaré muchos sitios.** Tengo ganas de ver los Picos de Europa.

Carmen: Y, ¿cuánto tiempo te quedarás en Asturias?

Estudiante: **Me quedaré unos quince días,** o sea, **volveré a mi casa** dentro de tres semanas, nada más. Estoy estudiando idiomas y vuelvo a clase el 21 de septiembre.

### *Vacations*

| | |
|---|---|
| **¿Cuándo piensas ir . . .?** | When do you think you'll go . . .? |
| **. . . de vacaciones?** | . . . on vacation? |
| **Pienso ir** | I'm thinking of going |
| **a principios de** | at the beginning of |
| **a fines de** | at the end of |
| **septiembre** | September (for months see p. 79) |
| **¿Adónde piensas ir?** | Where are you thinking of going? |
| **al extranjero** | abroad |
| **a las montañas/al mar** | to the mountains/to the sea |
| **al campo** | to the countryside |
| **Voy a alquilar un coche.** | I'm going to rent a car. |

| | |
|---|---|
| Visitaré muchos sitios. | I will visit many places. |
| Tengo ganas de ver . . . | I feel like seeing . . . |
| los Picos de Europa | the Asturian mountains |
| ¿Cuánto tiempo te quedarás? | How long will you stay? |
| Me quedaré unos quince días. | I'll stay about two weeks (a fortnight). |
| Volveré dentro de tres semanas. | I'll return within three weeks. |
| Volveremos a casa. | We'll return home. |
| Estoy estudiando idiomas. | I'm studying languages. |
| vuelvo a clase | I go back to class |

## Dates

| | |
|---|---|
| ¿En qué fecha estamos? | What's the date today? |
| el primero de mayo | May 1 |
| el cuatro de abril | April 4 |
| el veintiuno de septiembre | September 21 |
| sábado, diez de octubre | Saturday, October 10 |
| el mes pasado | last month |
| la semana próxima | next week |
| este año | this year |
| el cumpleaños | birthday |
| Navidad/Pascua | Christmas/Easter |
| ayer/hoy/mañana | yesterday/today/tomorrow |
| todos los días | every day |
| (días) laborables | work days |
| (días) festivos | public holidays, feast days |

# ENTERTAINMENT

Going to the movies   In the city, movie theaters generally have three showings: one at about 4:30 pm, the next at about 7:30 pm, and the last at about 10 or 11 pm. You may find a continuous session (**sesión continua**) starting at about 4 or 5 pm. In the country, there may only be two sessions (**función de la tarde** and **función de la noche**). Many foreign films are shown and most are dubbed into Spanish. When they are shown in the original language with subtitles, this is indicated by **V.O.** (**versión original**). It is customary to tip the usher (**acomodador/a**).

## SESIÓN CONTINUA

**Cristal.** (2) / ☎ 234 93 53 / Bravo Murillo, 120; Cuatro Caminos / *Metro* Cuatro Caminos.
—**Luna de lobos y Superdetective en Hollywood II.** No recomendadas para menores de 13 años. Continua desde las 4.35 de la tarde.
**España.** (3) / ☎ 269 56 70 / General Ricardos, 4 / *Metro* Marqués de Vadillo. Autobús 34.
—**Cuenta conmigo y Nadine.** Toleradas. 4.30.
**Espronceda.** (4) / ☎ 441 92 51 / Alonso Cano, 28; Chamberí / *Metro* Ríos Rosas.
—**Las nuevas aventuras de Popeye y Superman IV.** Laborables, continua, 5; sábados y festivos, 4.30. Toleradas.
**Europa.** (3) / ☎ 233 10 48 / Bravo Murillo, 160; Tetuán / *Metro* Estrecho.

## ¿qué te gustaría hacer?/what would you like to do?

Felipe invites Luisa to go out with him but they don't know where to go . . .

Felipe: **¿Qué vamos a hacer esta noche?**

Luisa: Pues, no sé. **¿Te gustaría ir a una discoteca?**

Felipe: No, bailar no me gusta nada.

Luisa: Entonces, **¿qué te gusta hacer en tu tiempo libre?**

Felipe: **Me gusta ir al cine,** me gusta salir con amigos, me gusta escuchar música. Y tú, **¿cuáles son tus aficiones?**

Luisa: Es difícil. Me gusta bailar, me gusta mucho ir al teatro y también me gusta escuchar música. **Me encanta la música pop.**

Felipe: Ésa no me gusta. **Prefiero la música clásica.** Toco el piano y estoy aprendiendo la flauta.

Luisa: Pues, mira. **¿por qué no vamos al cine?**

Felipe: Buena idea. ¿Sabes qué películas ponen en este momento?

Luisa: No. Hay que mirar la cartelera.

### Going out or staying in?

| Spanish | English |
|---|---|
| ¿Qué te gusta hacer? | What do you like doing? |
| ¿Qué vamos a hacer? | What shall we do? |
| ¿Te gustaría ir a . . .? | Would you like to go to . . .? |
| ¿Qué te parece ir a . . .? | What do you think of going to . . .? |
| No puedo salir esta tarde. | I can't go out this evening. |
| Buena idea. | Good idea. |
| Me gustaría mucho. | I would like to very much. |
| Me encantaría. | I would love to. |
| No tengo ganas. | I don't feel like it. |
| Bailar no me gusta nada. | I don't like dancing at all. |
| tu tiempo libre | your free time |
| Me gusta . . . | I like . . . |
| ir al cine/al teatro | going to the movies/theater |
| salir con amigos | going out with friends |
| ir a los toros | going to a bullfight |
| escuchar música | listening to music |
| bailar | dancing |
| pasear/dar paseos | going for walks |
| ver la televisión | watching television |
| leer | reading |
| ¿Cuáles son tus aficiones? | What are your hobbies? |
| Es difícil. | It's difficult. |

### Listening to or playing music

| Spanish | English |
|---|---|
| Me encanta . . . | I adore . . . |
| la música pop | pop music |

| la música clásica | classical music |
|---|---|
| ir a un concierto | going to a concert |
| la orquesta/el cantante | orchestra/singer |
| Toco el piano/la flauta/el violín/ el clarinete/la trompeta/la guitarra | I play the piano/flute/violin/ the clarinet/trumpet/guitar |
| Estoy aprendiendo | I am learning |

## Going to the movies

| ¿Por qué no vamos al cine? | Why don't we go to the movies? |
|---|---|
| una película | film |
| ¿Sabes qué películas ponen? | Do you know what films are showing? |
| en este momento | at the moment |
| V.O. subtitulada | original version with subtitles |
| sesión continua | continuous performance |
| Autorizada para todos los públicos | Suitable for everyone |
| No recomendada para menores de 18 años | Not recommended for under 18 |
| Hay que mirar la cartelera | We'll have to look in the entertainment page |

## Buying a ticket for a show

| la taquilla | box office |
|---|---|
| asientos limitados | limited seating |
| la butaca/el anfiteatro | box seats/balcony |
| ¿Hay localidades para esta función? | Are there seats for this performance? |
| Localidades desde 250 pesetas | Seats from 250 pesetas |
| Dos entradas, por favor. | Two tickets, please. |
| ¿A qué hora empieza el espectáculo? | What time does the show start? |
| ¿Hay descuentos para estudiantes? | Are there student discounts? |
| la localidad, la entrada | ticket |
| venta anticipada | tickets in advance |

# the way it works

## I'm learning the flute

| Estoy estudiando | I am studying |
|---|---|
| Estoy aprendiendo | I am learning |

It's useful to be able to use the continuous present tense which is formed in a similar way to the English "I am . . . ing."
Use the present tense of **estar + present participle**, which is formed by taking the stem of the verb:

| escuch- and adding -ando | for -ar verbs |
|---|---|
| aprend- and adding -iendo | for -er and -ir verbs |

## The future tense

| **Visitaré** muchos sitios. | I will visit many places |
|---|---|
| **Me quedaré** quince días. | I will stay two weeks. |
| **Volveré** a mi casa. | I'll return home. |

These are examples of the future tense which is used as an alternative to **ir a +** infinitive: **Voy a** alquilar un coche.    I'm going to rent a car.

The future tense is formed normally by taking the infinitive and adding the following endings:

| | | | |
|---|---|---|---|
| visitar-**é** | I will visit | visitar-**emos** | we will visit |
| visitar-**ás** | you will visit | visitar-**éis** | you will visit |
| visitar-**á** | he/she will visit | visitar-**án** | they will visit |
| | you will visit (formal) | | you will visit (formal) |

These endings are the same for all verbs but some verbs form the future stem from a variation of the infinitive. Some common examples are:

| | | | |
|---|---|---|---|
| salir: | to go out | sal**dré** | I will go out |
| tener: | to have | ten**dré** | I will have |
| hay: | there is | ha**brá** | there will be |

## things to do

**6.6**  **¿Cuáles son tus aficiones?** What do you like doing in your spare time?

Me encanta  me gusta mucho  me gusta  no me gusta nada

| *En casa* | *Por la tarde* | *De vacaciones* |
|---|---|---|
| **1** ver la televisión | salir con amigos | ir a las montañas |
| **2** jugar a las cartas | ir al cine | ir a la playa |
| **3** leer | ir al teatro | visitar muchos sitios |
| **4** escuchar la música | ir a un restaurante | hacer el esquí |
| **5** cocinar (to cook) | ir a una discoteca | ir al extranjero |

**6.7**  **1** What is being advertised here?
**2** What does the ad say about César Delgado and Teresa del Sol?
**3** What days of the week is it open?
**4** What times of day?
**5** Where is the exhibition held?

**la exposición**    exhibition
**la ceramista**    ceramic artist

**GALERÍAS DE ARTE**
**EXPOSICIONES**
**Ateneo de Madrid.** Sala de exposiciones Santa Catalina / Santa Catalina, 10.
—Exposición de **César Delgado**, pintor, y **Teresa del Sol**, ceramista. De lunes a sábados, de 18 a 20 horas.

**6.8**  You want to buy tickets for a theater performance.

**1** Ask if there are any tickets for tonight.
**2** Ask the price of the tickets.
**3** Say you would like two tickets.
**4** Ask how much it comes to.
**5** Ask what time the show starts.

# USING THE TELEPHONE

You can now make a direct phone call to another country from all big cities and towns and most tourist centers in Spain. Look for a telephone booth marked **Teléfono Internacional.** To operate, insert a 50-peseta coin, lift the receiver, wait for the dial tone, dial 07, wait for a higher tone, then dial the code of the country you are calling, followed by the local area code and then the number. Be prepared—bring a lot of coins with you!

## una llamada telefónica/a telephone call

Luisa suggests it might be a good idea to telephone Pilar to let her know when they are returning to Madrid.

Luisa:  ¿Oye, Juan, vas a llamar a tu madre?
Juan:   Sí, sí, la llamaré ahora misma.
Luisa:  **¿Cuál es tu número?** Voy a marcarlo si quieres.
Juan:   Es el 33-78-92.
Luisa:  (dials the number) Aquí tienes. (Juan takes over)
Pilar:  **Diga.**
Juan:   **Hola, mamá. Soy yo,** Juan. ¿Qué tal?
Pilar:  Hola. ¿Qué hay? ¿Qué tal Luisa y Miguel? ¿Qué estáis haciendo? ¿Cuándo vais a volver a Madrid?

| Juan: | Pues, estamos muy bien . . . Llegamos el miércoles por la tarde, . . . el jueves Luisa y Miguel se dieron una vuelta por Santander y compraron unas cosas. . . . El sábado yo fui con Miguel a un partido de fútbol y Luisa fue en coche con un amigo mío a . . . algún sitio. ¿Adónde fuiste, Luisa? |
| Luisa: | A muchos sitios—a Cangas de Onís y . . . |
| Juan: | (to Pilar) Fueron a Cangas de Onís. Y por la noche se fueron al cine. En fin, lo estamos pasando muy bien. |
| Pilar: | ¿Con quién salió Luisa? ¿Con Martín? |
| Juan: | No . . . con Felipe. Es un buen chico, sabes, muy serio. |
| Pilar: | ¡Ah, sí! Me acuerdo . . . Bueno, y ¿cuándo pensáis volver? |
| Juan: | A lo mejor, mañana. Cogeremos el tren de las once y media y llegaremos a eso de las seis de la tarde. |
| Pilar: | Muy bien. Entonces, hasta mañana. |
| Juan: | **Adiós, mamá.** |

## Telephone talk

| | |
|---|---|
| **llamar por teléfono** | to telephone |
| **¿Cuál es tu/su número?** | What's your number? |
| **Mi número de teléfono es . . .** | My telephone number is . . . |
| **Quiero hablar con . . .** | I want to speak to . . . |
| **marcar** | to dial |
| **Diga, Dígame** | Hello (when picking up receiver) |
| **¿Quién habla?** | Who's speaking? |
| **¿De parte de quién?** | Who's calling? |
| **Llamo de parte de . . .** | I'm calling for . . . |
| **Soy . . .** | It's . . . (+ speaker's name) |
| **Hable más despacio/lento.** | Speak more slowly. |
| **No entiendo.** | I don't understand. |
| **¿Quiere dejarle algún recado?** | Do you want to leave him a message? |
| **¿Quiere decirle que . . .?** | Please tell him that . . . |
| **la guía telefónica** | telephone directory |
| **el teléfono internacional** | international telephone |
| **el prefijo** | area code |
| **el cobro revertido** | reverse charge (collect) call |

## Saying what you did

| | |
|---|---|
| **Llegamos el miércoles.** | We arrived on Wednesday. |
| **dieron una vuelta por Santander** | they walked around Santander |
| **compraron unas cosas** | they bought some things |
| **Yo fui a un partido de fútbol.** | I went to a soccer match. |

| | |
|---|---|
| Carmen fue en coche a . . . | Carmen drove to . . . |
| algún sitio | some place |
| ¿Adónde fuisteis? | Where did you go? |
| Fuimos a Cangas de Onís. | We went to Cangas de Onís. |
| se fueron al cine | they went to the movies |
| ¿Con quién salió Luisa? | Who did Luisa go out with? |
| Un buen chico, muy serio | A good young man, very serious |
| Sí, me acuerdo | Yes, I remember |

## the way it works

### Saying what you are doing

| | |
|---|---|
| ¿Qué estáis haciendo? | What are you doing? |
| Lo estamos pasando muy bien. | We are having a good time. |

### Saying what you intend to do

| | |
|---|---|
| Le llamaré ahora mismo. | I'll call her at once. |
| ¿Cuándo pensáis volver? | When do you intend to come back? |
| A lo mejor, mañana. | Probably tomorrow. |
| Cogeremos el tren. | We'll catch the train. |
| Llegaremos a eso de las seis. | We'll arrive about six. |

### Saying what happened

| | |
|---|---|
| Fui a un partido de fútbol. | I went to a soccer match. |
| ¿Adónde fuiste? | Where did you go? |

**llegamos** (we arrived), **pasearon** (they walked around), **compraron** (they bought), **salió** (she went out).

All these verbs are in the **preterite** tense, which is used a great deal in Spanish for relating past events. The endings for this tense are as follows:

**-ar** verbs, e.g., **comprar** (to buy)

| | | | |
|---|---|---|---|
| compré | I bought | compramos | we bought |
| compraste | you bought (fam.) | comprasteis | you bought (fam.) |
| compró | he/she/you bought | compraron | they/you bought |

**-er** verbs, e.g., **volver** (to return)

| | | | |
|---|---|---|---|
| volví | I returned | volvimos | we returned |
| volviste | you returned (fam.) | volvisteis | you returned (fam.) |
| volvió | he/she/you returned | volvieron | they/you returned |

**-ir** verbs, e.g., **salir** (to leave)

| | | | |
|---|---|---|---|
| salí | I left | salimos | we left |
| saliste | you left (fam.) | salistesi | you left (fam.) |
| salió | he/she/you left | salieron | they/you left |

69

A number of verbs are irregular in the preterite. Here are three common ones:

**dar** (to give)

| | | | |
|---|---|---|---|
| **di** | I gave | **dimos** | we gave |
| **diste** | you gave | **disteis** | you gave |
| **dio** | he/she gave, you gave | **dieron** | they gave, you gave |

**ir** (to go) *and* **ser** (to be) (**ir** and **ser** share the same pattern)

| | | | |
|---|---|---|---|
| **fui** | I went | **fuimos** | we went |
| **fuiste** | you went | **fuisteis** | you went |
| **fue** | he/she went, you went | **fueron** | they went, you went |

**hacer** (to do, make)

| | | | |
|---|---|---|---|
| **hice** | I made | **hicimos** | we made |
| **hiciste** | you made | **hicisteis** | you made |
| **hizo** | he/she/it made, you made | **hicieron** | they made, you made |

Some verbs have a change in the spelling to enable them to keep the same stem sound throughout: **llegar** (to arrive), **llegué** (I arrived).

## things to do

**7.1** You are being interviewed about your daily routine.

| | |
|---|---|
| Interviewer: | ¿A qué hora se levanta? |
| You: | (I get up at 7:30) |
| Interviewer: | ¿Y qué hace después? |
| You: | (I have my breakfast) (use **desayunarse**) |
| Interviewer: | ¿A qué hora sale de la casa? |
| You: | (I leave at 9:00 and catch the bus to my office) |
| Interviewer: | ¿Vuelve a casa para almorzar? (to have lunch) |
| You: | (Yes, I come home at noon and have lunch. Then I do my shopping [**voy de compras**] and go back to the office in the afternoon) |

**7.2** The interviewer now wants to know what you did last Tuesday. Use the phrases from the previous exercise and put the verbs into the past tense:

| | | | |
|---|---|---|---|
| Interviewer: | El martes, ¿a qué hora se levantó? | You: | . . . . . . . . . . . . . . . . |
| Interviewer: | Y ¿qué hizo después? | You: | . . . . . . . . . . . . . . . . |
| Interviewer: | ¿A qué hora salió de la casa? | You: | . . . . . . . . . . . . . . . . |
| Interviewer: | ¿Volvió a casa para almorzar? | You: | . . . . . . . . . . . . . . . . |
| Interviewer: | ¿Qué hizo después? | You: | . . . . . . . . . . . . . . . . |

**7.3** Using the telephone. The telephone rings and you pick up the receiver. Can you take your part in a telephone conversation in which arrangements are being made?

| | |
|---|---|
| You: | [Hello] |
| Juan: | Hola, soy Juan. ¿Qué hay? Oye, quisiera invitarte a cenar esta tarde. Hoy es nuestra última noche en Santander, y mañana volvemos a Madrid. |
| You: | [Say you'd like to very much. Ask what time to come] |
| Juan: | Pues, a eso de las ocho. ¿Sabes dónde estamos? |
| You: | [Say yes, you know where he lives and you'll take a taxi] |
| Juan: | Bueno, entonces, hasta pronto. |

# DESCRIBING THINGS & PEOPLE

## ¿puede decirme cómo eran?/can you tell me what were they like?

Carmen has been asked to give a description of a couple she saw shoplifting.

| | |
|---|---|
| Policía: | **¿Cómo eran,** por favor? |
| Carmen: | Pues, mire, **había un chico y una chica.** El chico tenía unos veinte años, y la chica quizás veinticinco. |
| Policía: | **¿La chica era rubia o morena?** |
| Carmen: | **Era rubia y bastante baja. Tenía los ojos azules** y el pelo largo y rubio. |
| Policía: | Y, ¿qué llevaba? |
| Carmen: | Llevaba una falda negra muy corta, y un jersey verde. |
| Policía: | ¿Y el chico? |
| Carmen: | Era muy alto y moreno. **Llevaba vaqueros y botas** y una chaqueta de cuero. |
| Policía: | Muy bien. ¿Y a qué distancia de ellos estaba usted? |
| Carmen: | Estaba a unos tres metros, nada más. |
| Policía: | ¿Qué estaban haciendo? |
| Carmen: | Metían unos objetos en un bolso y de repente me vieron. Al verme se escaparon sin esperarse. |

### Describing what you saw

| | |
|---|---|
| ¿Cómo eran? | What did they look like? |
| Había un chico y una chica. | There were a boy and a girl. |
| tenía unos veinte años | he was about 20 |
| tenía quizás veinticinco | she perhaps 25 |
| ¿Era rubia o morena? | Was she blonde or brunette? |
| bastante baja | quite short |
| tenía los ojos azules/castaños | she had blue/brown eyes |
| el pelo largo | long hair |
| ¿Qué llevaba? | What was she wearing? |
| alto y moreno | tall and dark |
| llevaba vaqueros | he was wearing jeans |
| ¿A qué distancia de ellos estaba? | What distance away were you? |
| estaba a unos tres metros | I was about 3 meters away |
| Metían unos objetos | They were putting some things |
| en un bolso . . . | in a bag . . . |
| de repente me vieron | they suddenly caught sight of me |
| Al verme se escaparon | As soon as they saw me they fled |
| sin esperarse | in a flash (literally, "without waiting") |

71

## SAYING GOODBYE

### hasta el año que viene/see you next year

Juan's party is in full swing and all the guests are enjoying themselves.
They are out in the garden after supper.

Luisa: ¡Qué noche más estupenda! Lo hemos pasado muy bien aquí en España.

Felipe: **Siento mucho que no puedas quedarte en Santander.** Pero volverás el año próximo, ¿me prometes?

Luisa: Seguramente.

Felipe: ¿Qué cosas te gustan más en España?

Luisa: Pues, no hay problema. Hace buen tiempo todos los días, la gente es muy simpática, y **todo el mundo se divierte** mucho.

Felipe: Sí, es verdad. Pero, ¿qué pasa? ¡Está lloviendo! Y el pronóstico para mañana es malo—habrá tormentas. Eso no puede ser . . .

(They go inside, where Juan is being a good host.)

Juan: Hola, Felipe. ¿Quieres otra bebida?

Felipe: No, gracias, ya es tarde y tengo que irme. Oye, Juan, ¿por qué no vamos a Inglaterra en la primavera?

Juan: Me gustaría mucho. Estarás en Madrid la semana próxima, ¿verdad?

Felipe: Claro que sí. Bueno, pues te veré en Madrid. Muchas gracias y adiós a todos.

Juan: Adiós, hasta luego.

### *Party conversation*

| | |
|---|---|
| **¡Qué noche más estupenda!** | What a lovely evening! |
| **Lo hemos pasado muy bien.** | We have really enjoyed ourselves. |
| **Siento mucho que no puedas quedarte.** | I'm sorry you can't stay. |
| **Volverás el año próximo,** | You'll come back next year, |
| **¿me prometes?** | you promise me? |
| **seguramente/no hay problema** | certainly/no problem |
| **Hace buen tiempo** | It's good weather |
| **todos los días** | every day |
| **la gente es muy simpática** | people are nice |
| **todo el mundo se divierte** | everyone enjoys himself |
| **Sí, es verdad.** | Yes, it's true. |
| **¿Qué pasa?** | What's happening? |
| **Está lloviendo.** | It's raining. |
| **El pronóstico para mañana . . .** | The forecast for tomorrow . . . |
| **habrá tormentas** | there will be thunderstorms |
| **¡Eso no puede ser!** | That's not possible! |

| | |
|---|---|
| ¿Quieres otra bebida? | Do you want another drink? |
| Tengo que irme. | I have to go. |
| ¿Por qué no vamos a Inglaterra? | Why don't we go to England? |
| en la primavera | in the spring |
| Te veré en Madrid, ¿verdad? | I'll see you in Madrid, won't I? |
| Claro que sí. | Certainly. |
| Muchas gracias y adiós. | Many thanks and goodbye. |
| Adiós, hasta luego. | Goodbye, till then. |
| Hasta el año que viene. | See you next year. |

### The weather (El tiempo)

| | |
|---|---|
| ¿Qué tiempo hace? | What's the weather like? |
| Hace sol./Habrá sol. | It's sunny./There will be sunshine. |
| Hace frío/viento. | It's cold/windy. |
| Hace buen/mal tiempo. | It's good weather/bad weather. |
| Está nublado. | It's cloudy. |
| Está lloviendo/nevando. | It's raining/snowing. |
| Habrá temporal/tormenta. | There will be a gale/storm. |
| el cielo nuboso/cubierto | cloudy/overcast sky |
| el cielo despejado | clear sky |
| la lluvia/el chubasco | rain/shower |
| la nieve/el granizo/la niebla | snow/hail/fog |

## the way it works

### Saying what someone was like

| | |
|---|---|
| **Tenía** unos veinte años. | He was about 20. |
| **Era** rubia y bastante baja. | She was blonde and quite short. |
| **Estaba** a unos tres metros. | I was about 3 meters away. |

These are examples of the **imperfect** tense. This tense is mainly used for past descriptions of people and places, for saying what you or someone else was doing, or what was happening. It is usually formed by taking the stem of the verb and adding on endings as follows:

**-ar** verbs e.g., **llevar** (to wear, carry)

| | | | |
|---|---|---|---|
| llev-**aba** | I was wearing | llev-**ábamos** | we were wearing |
| llev-**abas** | you were wearing | llev-**abais** | you were wearing |
| llev-**aba** | he/she was wearing | llev-**aban** | they were wearing |
| | you were wearing | | you were wearing |

**-er** and **-ir** verbs share the same endings:

| | | | |
|---|---|---|---|
| ten-**ía** | I had | ten-**íamos** | we had |
| ten-**ías** | you had | ten-**íais** | you had |
| ten-**ía** | he/she had, you had | ten-**ían** | they had, you had |

A handful of verbs form the imperfect differently, among them **ser** (to be).

| | | | |
|---|---|---|---|
| **era** | I was | **éramos** | we were |
| **eras** | you were | **erais** | you were |
| **era** | he/she was, you were | **eran** | they were, you were |

The imperfect is often used in conjunction with the preterite when two things are happening at the same time: **Metían** unos objetos en un bolso cuando me **vieron**. (They were putting some things in a bag when they saw me.)

## Al verme . . .

**Al verme** se escaparon.     On seeing me, they escaped (ran away).

The use of **al + infinitive** is very common to join two verbs with the same subject: **Al acabar** sus estudios volvió a Madrid. (On finishing her studies, she returned to Madrid.)

## The weather is terrific!

**Hace** muy buen tiempo.     It's lovely weather.

**Hace** comes from **hacer** (to make) and is often used when talking about the weather. (See p. 46 for present-tense forms.)

## It's sunny every day!

**todos los** días     every day     **todo el** mundo     everyone

To say "all" or "every" use **todo, toda, todos, todas**.

## Really and truly

**verdaderamente** really **seguramente** surely **súbitamente** suddenly

To form an adverb you normally add **-mente** on to the feminine form of the adjective. Other common adverbs include:

**desgraciadamente** unluckily **afortunadamente** fortunately

## things to do

**7.4** What were you doing in Madrid? Some time ago you were living there and you are now being interviewed about it.

| Interviewer: | ¿Qué hacías en Madrid? |
|---|---|
| You: | [Say you were studying Spanish] |
| Interviewer: | ¿Dónde vivías? |
| You: | [Say you were living in the calle de Serrano with a family] |
| Interviewer: | ¿Había unos hijos en la familia? |
| You: | [Yes, there was a daughter] |
| Interviewer: | ¿Cómo se llamaba la hija y cuántos años tenía? |
| You: | [She was called Mari-Carmen and she was 23] |

| Interviewer: | ¿Qué hacías por la tarde? |
|---|---|
| You: | [You went out with friends, or sometimes you stayed at home and read, or watched television] |
| Interviewer: | En fin, ¿te gustaba Madrid? |
| You: | [Say yes, you liked it very much and you had a wonderful time] |

5  Miguel thinks he has lost his watch and he goes to the police station to report it. Look at the following interview and see if you can understand it:

| Miguel: | Buenas tardes. Creo que he perdido mi reloj en la calle. |
|---|---|
| Policía: | ¿Cuándo lo perdió, señor? |
| Miguel: | Pues, esta tarde fui al partido de fútbol y estoy seguro de que lo llevaba cuando salí del estadio. |
| Policía: | Sí, señor, pero ¿cuándo se dio usted cuenta de que lo había perdido? |
| Miguel: | Al llegar a mi casa me di cuenta de que no lo tenía. Lo busqué por todas partes pero no lo encontré. |
| Policía: | ¿El reloj era de gran valor, señor? |
| Miguel: | Pues, no sé exactamente, pero mi abuela me lo dio como regalo. |
| Policía: | Bueno, . . . ¿Quiere llenar este formulario, por favor, con todos los detalles, y veremos? . . . ¿Vive aquí en Santander? |
| Miguel: | No, mañana vuelvo a Madrid. |

### The language of losing something

| perder | to lose | He perdido | I have lost |
|---|---|---|---|
| robar | to steal | Me han robado | Someone has stolen |
| buscar | to look for | Busqué | I looked |
| encontrar | to find | No encontré | I didn't find |
| darse cuenta | to realize | Me di cuenta | I realized |
| el reloj | watch | la cartera | wallet |
| la bolsa | purse | la cámara | camera |

Now try to report what Miguel said, with the help of the following phrases:
Esta tarde, Miguel . . . a un partido de fútbol y . . . seguro de que lo . . . cuando . . . del estadio. Al llegar a su casa . . . cuenta de que no lo . . . Lo . . . por todas partes pero no lo . . .

**7.6**   **El pronóstico para mañana** (The forecast for tomorrow—showing that the weather in Spain isn't always perfect!)

*Cantábrico.* Cielo muy nuboso o cubierto con chubascos, que serán en forma de nieve en altitudes superiores a los 1.000 metros. Los vientos serán fuertes del noroeste. Habrá temporal fuerte con mar arbolada en la zona marítima. Máximas de 6°C y mínimas de −5°C.

1 Will the sky be clear or cloudy?
2 Will there be rain or snow showers?
3 What direction will the winds be from?
4 Where will there be a gale?
5 What will be the minimum temperature?

**7.7**   **¿Qué tiempo hace?** Here is a weather map of Spain. Can you say what the weather is like:

1 en el mar mediterráneo?
2 en los Pirineos?
3 en Madrid?
4 en el sur de España?
5 en el noroeste?

76

# EXERCISE KEY

**1.1** 1 Buenos días, señora. ¿Cómo está usted? 2 Buenas tardes, señor. ¿Cómo está? 3 Hola, ¿cómo estás?/Muy bien, gracias. 4 Hola, buenas tardes, ¿qué tal?
**1.2** Sí, soy Annie Rogers./Sí, éste es mi hermano, Felipe./Sí, es mi maleta./Sí, es su maleta.
**1.3** 1 ¿Es usted la señora Barillo? 2 ¿Es ésta su maleta? 3 ¿Dónde está? 4 ¿Cómo está usted? 5 ¿Cómo se llama su hermana?
**1.4** (Personal preferences).
**1.5** Thomas: un tinto, por favor. Alice: una coca-cola, por favor. Isabel: una taza de té con limón, por favor. Martín: Yo quiero una cerveza, por favor. You:
**1.6** ¿Qué bocadillos hay?/Uno de jamón, por favor./¿Qué helados hay?/Uno de fresa, por favor.
**1.7** 1 (c). 2 (e). 3 (d). 4 (a). 5 (b).

**2.1** 1 (d). 2 (f). 3 (a). 4 (e). 5 (b). 6 (c).
**2.2** 1 Yo también hablo el inglés. 2 Yo también estudio idiomas. 3 Yo también trabajo en Londres. 4 Nosotros también hablamos el español. 5 Nosotros también estudiamos el español.
**2.3** 1 Se llama Eduardo. Es español de Madrid. Es contable. Tiene veinticuatro años. Es bajo y gordo. Tiene un hermano.
**2.4** 1 Yo vivo en Madrid. ¿Dónde vive usted? 2 Yo vivo en Tarragona, pero mi hermano vive en Valencia. 3 Nosotros vivimos en Toledo. Y vosotros, ¿dónde vivís? 4 Y ellos, ¿dónde viven? ¿En Salamanca? No, viven en Ciudad Real.
**2.5** 1 Son las cuatro. 2 Son las cuatro y cuarto. 3 Son las cuatro y veinte. 4 Son las cuatro y diez. 5 Son las cinco menos cuarto. 6 Son las cinco menos veinte. 7 Son las tres y media. 8 Son las cinco menos veinticinco.
**2.6** 1 Hay uno a las once veinticinco. 2 Hay uno a las quince treinta. 3 Hay uno a las cinco cuarenta y cinco. 4 Hay uno a las nueve treinta. 5 Hay uno a las diez treinta y cinco.
**2.7** 1 Son tres mil setecientas pesetas. 2 Son siete mil quinientas pesetas. 3 Son cuatro mil quinientas pesetas.
**2.8** (a) ¿A qué hora sale el próximo tren para Sevilla?/¿A qué hora llega a Sevilla? (b) Uno, por favor./¿Qué línea es para Colón?/¿Tengo que hacer transbordo?

**3.1** 2 Sí, es verde. 3 No, es blanca. Es de algodón. 4 No, es azul. Es de lana. 5 Sí, son grises.
**3.2** Quisiera una camiseta./La cuarenta./Me gusta el estilo pero no me gusta el color./Me gusta más la azul. ¿Puedo probármela?/Me parece bien. ¿Cuánto es, por favor?/Bueno, la compro.
**3.3** 1 No, es demasiado pequeño. ¿Hay otro más grande?/2 No, es demasiado larga. ¿Hay otra más corta?/3 No, es demasiado grande. ¿Hay otro más pequeño?/4 Son demasiado cortos. ¿Hay otros más largos?/5 Son demasiado pequeños. ¿Hay otros más grandes?
**3.4** Belt: dos mil setecientas pesetas. Purse: nueve mil doscientas pesetas. Guitar: seis mil quinientas pesetas. Perfum: ochocientas pesetas. Necklace: doce mil seiscientas pesetas.
**3.5** 1 (c). 2 (f). 3 (d). 4 (b). 5 (a). 6 (e).
**3.6** 1 (e). 2 (h). 3 (d). 4 (g). 5 (b). 6 (c). 7 (f). 8 (a).
**3.7** 250 gramos de mantequilla; 1 litro de leche; 500 gramos de jamón de York; 1 paquete de galletas; 1 lata de sardinas; 1 kilo de plátanos; ½ kilo de melocotones; 6 peras maduras; 1 litro de aceite; 2 botellas de vino tinto; 12 huevos
**3.8** el café: ciento noventa ptas; 12 huevos: ciento noventa ptas; los plátanos: cien ptas; los tomates: trescientas ptas. Total: setecientas ochenta ptas.
**3.9** Doscientos gramos de queso y cien gramos de jamón serrano, por favor./medio kilo de manzanas y seis plátanos maduros./Un litro de leche, por favor. Eso es todo. ¿Cuánto es, por favor?
**3.10** Buenos días, quisiera cambiar unos dólares, por favor./Ciento cincuenta dólares. ¿A cómo está el cambio hoy?/Deme dos billetes de cinco mil, tres billetes de mil y uno de quinientas pesetas.
**3.11** Quiero dos de estos pasteles y una tarta, por favor./Sí, deme un donut y un panecillo./No, es para llevar.

# EXERCISE KEY

**4.1** Tome la primera calle a la izquierda. 2 Coja la segunda calle a la derecha. 3 Siga todo derecho. 4 Siga hasta el final de esta calle, y doble a la derecha.

**4.2** 1 La Catedral. 2 El Banco de España. 3 La Oficina de Turismo. 4 La Aduana. 5 La Plaza de Toros.

**4.3** 1 Lleno de super, por favor. 2 treinta y cinco litros de super, p.f. 3 ¿Quiere comprobar el aceite, p.f.? 4 ¿Quiere comprobar la presión, p.f.?

**4.4** 1 Mi coche no quiere arrancar. 2 El contacto no funciona. 3 ¿Puede mandar un mecánico, p.f.? 4 ¿Cuánto tiempo tardará?

**4.5** Me duele el estómago y tengo diarrea./Desde hace una semana./ Muchas gracias, adiós.

**4.6** ¿Puede darme algo para las picaduras de insecto?/Quiero un paquete de esparadrapos y unas pastillas para la garganta, p.f.

**5.1** 1 Quiero una habitación doble. 2 . . . sencilla. 3 . . . con ducha. 4 . . . con baño. 5 . . . con dos camas.

**5.2** Buenas tardes, he reservado una habitación./Me llamo . . ./Está en el coche./Muchas gracias.

**5.3** ¿Tiene una habitación?/No, sólo con lavabo./¿Cuánto es una habitación con baño?/Lo siento, es demasiado caro.

**5.4** Buenas tardes. ¿Hay sitio, por favor?/Somos cuatro y tenemos una caravana./Una semana.

**5.5** 1 ¿Hay piscina? 2 ¿ . . . duchas calientes? 3 ¿ . . . .supermercado? 4 ¿ . . . .restaurante? 5 ¿ . . . .Correos?

**5.6** 1 No funcionan las duchas calientes. 2 No funcionan los retretes. 3 No funciona la electricidad. 4 No funciona el grifo. 5 No funciona el agua potable.

**5.7** (choice of menus)

**5.8** De primero, los mejillones./Pues, voy a tomar la sopa de pescado./De segundo, la merluza al horno./Entonces, ¿hay filete de lenguado?/Una naranja, por favor./Vale. Un plátano, por favor. La cuenta, por favor.

**6.1** Me gusta el tenis y la natación./ No, no me gusta nada./Sí, pero prefiero el tenis.

**6.2** Luisa: Me gusta el tenis, el baloncesto, el voleibol y el golf. Juan: Me gusta la natación, la vela, el windsurf y la pesca.

**6.3** (a) Dos entradas, por favor./Son doscientas cincuenta pesetas./¿A qué hora están abiertas?/Se abren a las tres de la tarde. (b) Dos entradas, por favor./ Son ciento cincuenta pesetas./¿A qué hora se cierra?/Se cierra a las ocho.

**6.4** 1 (d). 2 (e). 3 (b). 4 (a). 5 (c).

**6.5** 2 ¿Conoce usted a Conchita, una amiga de mi esposa? 3 ¿Sabe jugar al ajedrez? 4 ¿Sabe usted cuándo se termina la reunión? 5 Sé que a mi esposa le gustaría mucho conocerle.

**6.6** (personal preferences)

**6.7** 1 Art Exhibition. 2 Delgado is a painter; Teresa del Sol is a ceramist. 3 Open from Monday to Saturday. 4 From 6 pm to 8 pm. 5 10, Santa Catalina Street.

**6.8** 1 ¿Quedan localidades para la función de esta noche? 2 ¿Qué precio tienen las localidades? 3 Quisiera dos entradas, por favor. 4 ¿Cuánto es, por favor? 5 ¿A qué hora empieza el espectáculo?

**7.1** Me levanto a las siete y media./Me desayuno./Salgo a las nueve y voy en autobús a mi oficina./Sí, vuelvo a casa al mediodía para almorzar. Después, voy de compras y vuelvo a la oficina por la tarde.

**7.2** Me levanté a las siete y media./Me desayuné./Salí a las nueve y fui en autobús a mi oficina./Volví a casa al mediodía para almorzar. Después fui de compras, y entonces volví a la oficina por la tarde.

**7.3** Dígame./Me gustaría mucho. ¿A qué hora vendré? Sí, sé donde vives y cogeré un taxi.

**7.4** Estudiaba el español./Vivía en la calle de Serrano con una familia española./Sí, había una hija./Se llamaba Mari-Carmen y tenía veintitrés años./ Salía con unos amigos, o me quedaba en casa y leía, o miraba la televisión./Sí, me gustaba mucho. Lo pasaba muy bien.

**7.5** Fue . . . estaba . . . tenía . . . salió . . .

se dio . . . tenía . . . buscó . . . encontró
**7.6** 1 Cloudy. 2 Snow at high altitudes.
3 NW. 4 The coast. 5 −5°C.
**7.7** 1 Está despejado con olas de un
metro. 2 Hay tormentas. 3 Está muy
nuboso. 4 Hay nubes alternas. Hace
mucho calor. 5 Está muy nuboso con
lluvias y posibilidad de tormentas.

# English–Spanish topic vocabularies

## Numbers 0–100

| 0 | cero | | | | | | |
|---|------|---|------|---|-------------|-----|------------------|
| 1 | uno/una | 11 | once | 21 | veintiuno | 31 | treinta y uno |
| 2 | dos | 12 | doce | 22 | veintidós | 32 | treinta y dos |
| 3 | tres | 13 | trece | 23 | veintitrés | | etc. |
| 4 | cuatro | 14 | catorce | 24 | veinticuatro | 40 | cuarenta |
| 5 | cinco | 15 | quince | 25 | veinticinco | 50 | cincuenta |
| 6 | seis | 16 | dieciséis | 26 | veintiséis | 60 | sesenta |
| 7 | siete | 17 | diecisiete | 27 | veintisiete | 70 | setenta |
| 8 | ocho | 18 | dieciocho | 28 | veintiocho | 80 | ochenta |
| 9 | nueve | 19 | diecinueve | 29 | veintinueve | 90 | noventa |
| 10 | diez | 20 | veinte | 30 | treinta | 100 | cien, ciento |

## Numbers 101–1000

| 101 | ciento uno | 500 | quinientos/as | first | primero/a |
|-----|------------|-----|---------------|-------|-----------|
| 150 | ciento cincuenta | 600 | seiscientos/as | second | segundo/a |
| 200 | doscientos/as | 700 | setecientos/as | third | tercero/a |
| 250 | doscientos cincuenta | 800 | ochocientos/as | fourth | cuarto/a |
| 300 | trescientos/as | 900 | novecientos/as | fifth | quinto/a |
| 400 | cuatrocientos/as | 1000 | mil | sixth | sexto/a |
| | | | | seventh | séptimo/a |

| | | | | | |
|---|---|---|---|---|---|
| 1,500 | **mil quinientos/as** | ground floor | **planta baja** | eighth | octavo/a |
| 2,000 | **dos mil** | 1st floor | **primer piso** | ninth | noveno/a |
| 20,000 | **veinte mil** | 3rd floor | **tercer piso** | tenth | décimo/a |
| 7,300 | **siete mil trescientos** | | | | |

## The calendar and seasons

**The months** (los meses del año)

| | | | |
|---|---|---|---|
| January | **enero** | July | **julio** |
| *The seasons* (las temporadas) | | February | **febrero** | August | **agosto** |
| Spring | **la primavera** | March | **marzo** | September | **septiembre** |
| Summer | **el verano** | April | **abril** | October | **octubre** |
| Autumn | **el otoño** | May | **mayo** | November | **noviembre** |
| Winter | **el invierno** | June | **junio** | December | **diciembre** |

Friday, February 2  **viernes, dos de febrero**
last week/next month  **la semana pasada/el próximo mes**

# VOCABULARY

## Professions

| | | | |
|---|---|---|---|
| accountant | contable | housewife | ama de casa |
| architect | arquitecto/a | journalist | periodista |
| businessman | hombre de negocios | lawyer | abogado/a |
| businesswoman | mujer de negocios | manager | director/a/gerente |
| civil servant | funcionario/a | nurse | enfermero/a |
| computer operator | operario/a de computadoras | plumber | fontanero/a |
| | | policeman | policía |
| dentist | dentista | sales clerk | dependiente/a |
| designer | diseñador/ora | salesman | representante |
| doctor | médico/a | secretary | secretario/a |
| employee | empleado/a | social worker | asistente social |
| engineer | ingeniero/a | teacher | profesor/ora |
| farmer | agricultor/ora | technician | técnico/a |
| electrician | electricista | unemployed | desempleado/a |

## Clothes (la ropa) and accessories

| | |
|---|---|
| . . . for women | . . . para mujeres |
| . . . for men | . . . para hombres |
| . . . for children | . . . para jóvenes |
| . . . for babies | . . . para niños |
| bag | el bolso |
| bathing suit | el traje de baño |
| belt | el cinturón |
| blouse | la blusa |
| bra | el sostén |
| briefs/pants | los calzoncillos |
| coat | el abrigo |
| dress | el vestido |
| gloves | los guantes |
| handkerchief | el pañuelo |
| hat | el sombrero |
| jacket | la chaqueta |
| jeans | los vaqueros |
| jumper (pullover) | el jersey |
| raincoat | el impermeable |
| scarf | la bufanda |
| (head)scarf | el pañuelo de cabeza |
| shirt | la camisa |
| shorts | los pantalones cortos |
| skirt | la falda |
| sleeves | las mangas |
| socks | los calcetines |
| stockings | las medias |
| suit | el traje |
| sweater | el suéter |
| tights | el panty |
| trousers | los pantalones |
| t-shirt | la camiseta |

## Shoes

| | |
|---|---|
| boots | las botas |
| sandals | las sandalias |
| shoes | los zapatos |
| slippers | las zapatillas |

## Colors

| | |
|---|---|
| color | el color |
| black | negro/a |
| blue | azul |
| brown | marrón |
| green | verde |
| grey | gris |
| red | rojo/a |
| white | blanco/a |
| yellow | amarillo/a |
| dark, light | oscuro/a, claro/a |

## Materials

| | |
|---|---|
| acrylic | el acrílico |
| cotton | elalgodón |
| denim | el dril |
| leather | el cuero |
| nylon | el nilón |
| silk | la seda |
| suede | el ante |
| velvet | el terciopelo |
| wool | la lana |

*Note:* You say: una falda **de** seda ( = a skirt made of silk), and pantalones gris**es**, negr**os**, etc.; camisetas blanc**as**

# VOCABULARY

## Pharmaceutical items, etc.

| | |
|---|---|
| aspirins | las aspirinas |
| bandage | la venda |
| band-aid | el esparadrapo |
| contraceptive pill | la píldora |
| cotton-wool | el algodón |
| insect repellent | el repelente para insectos |
| lozenges (throat) | las pastillas |
| pill, tablet | el comprimido |
| sleeping pill | el somnífero |

## Toiletries and other items

| | |
|---|---|
| baby food | el alimento para bebé |
| comb | la peine |
| condoms | los condones |
| contraceptives | los anticonceptivos |
| diapers | los pañales |
| lipstick | el lápiz de labios |
| pacifier | el chupete |
| perfume | el perfume |
| razor blades | las hojas de afeitar |
| sanitary napkins | las compresas |
| shampoo | el champú |
| shaving cream | la crema de afeitar |
| soap | el jabón |
| sunglasses | las gafas de sol |
| suntan lotion | la crema bronceadora |
| tampons | los tampones |
| tissues | los pañuelos de papel |
| toilet paper | el papel higiénico |
| toothbrush | el cepillo de dientes |
| toothpaste | la pasta de dientes |

## Food shops

| | |
|---|---|
| bakery | la panadería |
| butcher shop | la carnicería |
| pastry shop | la pastelería |
| confectionery | la confitería |
| dairy | la lechería |
| delicatessen | la mantequería |
| fish store | la pescadería |
| fruit shop | la frutería |
| grocery store | la tienda de alimentación, comestibles |
| market | el mercado |
| produce store | la verdulería |
| supermarket | el supermercado |
| wine merchant | la tienda de vinos, la bodega |

## Tobacco shop (el estanco)

| | |
|---|---|
| cigar | el puro |
| cigarette | el cigarrillo |
| matches | los fósforos, las cerillas |
| newspaper | el periódico |
| magazine | la revista |
| postcard | la (tarjeta) postal |
| stamp | el sello |
| tobacco | el tabaco |
| (Virginian, black) | rubio, negro |

## Shops (las tiendas) and departments

| | |
|---|---|
| bank | el banco |
| bookstore | la librería |
| camping equipment | el equipo de camping |
| clothes shop | la tienda de ropa |
| cosmetics, etc | la perfumería |
| dry cleaner's | la tintorería |
| hairdresser | la peluquería |
| hardware store | la ferretería |
| household (cleaning) | la droguería |
| newsstand | el quiosco |
| pharmacy | la farmacia |
| post office | el correos |
| shoe shop | la zapatería |
| stationery store | la papelería |
| tobacco shop | el estanco |
| toy store | la juguetería |

## Fish (el pescado), Shellfish (los mariscos)

| | |
|---|---|
| anchovy | la anchoa |
| bass | la lubina |
| bream | el besugo |
| clams | las almejas |
| cod | el bacalao |
| crab | el cangrejo |
| hake | la merluza |
| lobster | la langosta |
| mussels | los mejillones |
| octopus | el pulpo |
| prawns | los langostinos |
| red mullet | el salmonete |
| salmon | el salmón |
| sardine | la sardina |
| shrimp | las gambas |
| skate | la raya |
| sole | el lenguado |
| squid | los calamares |
| trout | la trucha |
| tuna | el atún |

# VOCABULARY

## Fruit (la fruta)

| | |
|---|---|
| apple | la manzana |
| apricot | el albaricoque |
| banana | el plátano |
| cherry | la cereza |
| dates | los dátiles |
| grapes | las uvas |
| fig | el higo |
| lemon | el limón |
| melon | el melón |
| nuts | las avellanas |
| orange | la naranja |
| peach | el melocotón |
| pear | la pera |
| pineapple | la piña |
| plum | la ciruela |
| raspberry | la frambuesa |
| strawberry | la fresa |
| watermelon | la sandía |

## Vegetables (las verduras)

| | |
|---|---|
| artichoke | la alcachofa |
| asparagus | los espárragos |
| beans (broad) | las habas |
| beans (French) | los frijoles |
| cabbage | la berza |
| carrots | las zanahorias |
| cauliflower | la coliflor |
| garlic | el ajo |
| lettuce | la lechuga |
| mushroom | el champiñón |
| olives | las aceitunas |
| onion | la cebolla |
| peas (chick) | los garbanzos |
| peas (green) | los guisantes |
| pepper (sweet) | el pimiento |
| potato | la patata |
| salad | la ensalada |
| tomato | el tomate |

## Meat (la carne), Poultry (las aves)

| | |
|---|---|
| beef | la carne de res |
| chicken | el pollo |
| ham | el jamón |
| lamb | el cordero |
| pork | el cerdo |
| rabbit | el conejo |
| sausage | el salchichón |
| sausages | las salchichas |
| veal | la ternera |

## Bread, etc.

| | |
|---|---|
| bread, loaf | el pan |
| bread roll | el panecillo |
| cake, pastry | el pastel |
| doughnut | el donut; el churro |
| tart, cake | la tarta, la torta |

## Groceries

| | |
|---|---|
| biscuits, crackers | los bizcochos, las galletas |
| butter | la mantequilla |
| cheese | el queso |
| coffee | el café |
| eggs | los huevos |
| flour | la harina |
| margarine | la margarina |
| milk | la leche |
| oil | el aceite |
| pasta | la pasta |
| pepper | la pimienta |
| rice | el arroz |
| salt | la sal |
| sugar | el azúcar |
| tea | el té |
| vinegar | el vinagre |

## Parts of the car

| | |
|---|---|
| battery | la batería |
| brake(s) | el freno, los frenos |
| carburetor | el carburador |
| clutch | el embrague |
| engine | el motor |
| exhaust | el tubo de escape |
| fanbelt | la correa de ventilador |
| headlight | el faro |
| ignition | el contacto |
| indicator | el intermitente |
| wheel | la rueda, el volante |
| windshield | el parabrisas |
| wipers | los limpiaparabrisas |

## Parts of the body

| | |
|---|---|
| ankle | el tobillo |
| arm | el brazo |
| back | la espalda |
| blood | la sangre |
| bone | el hueso |
| chest | el pecho |
| ear | la oreja, el oído |
| elbow | el codo |
| eye | el ojo |
| face | la cara |
| finger | el dedo |
| foot | el pie |
| hair | el pelo, los cabellos |

# VOCABULARY

| | |
|---|---|
| hand | la mano |
| head | la cabeza |
| heart | el corazón |
| knee | la rodilla |
| leg | la pierna |
| lung | el pulmón |
| mouth | la boca |
| muscle | el músculo |
| nose | la nariz |
| rib | la costilla |
| shoulder | el hombro |
| skin | la piel |
| stomach | el estómago |
| throat | la garganta |
| thumb | el pulgar |
| tooth | el diente |
| toe | el dedo del pie |
| wrist | la muñeca |

## Places to visit and natural features

| | |
|---|---|
| bridge | el puente |
| building | el edificio |
| castle | el castillo, el alcázar |
| cathedral | la catedral |
| church | la iglesia |
| cloister | el claustro |
| house | la casa |
| monastery | el monasterio |
| mosque | la mezquita |
| museum | el museo |
| palace | el palacio |
| wall | el muro |
| cave | la cueva |
| hill | la colina |
| island | la isla |
| lake | el lago |
| mountain | la montaña |
| mountain range | la sierra |
| river | el río |
| sea | el mar |
| valley | el valle |

## Souvenirs (los recuerdos)

| | |
|---|---|
| bull | el toro |
| castanets | las castañuelas |
| doll | la muñeca |
| fan | el abanico |
| necklace | el collar |
| pottery | la cerámica |
| pottery jug | el botijo |

## Sports and games

| | |
|---|---|
| archery | el tiro con arco |
| athletics | el atletismo |
| basketball | el baloncesto |
| cards | las cartas |
| chess | el ajedrez |
| cycling | el ciclismo |
| fishing | la pesca |
| golf | el golf |
| horse riding | la equitación |
| judo | el yudo |
| jogging | el footing |
| rowing | el remo |
| sailing | la vela |
| shooting | la caza |
| soccer | el fútbol |
| swimming | la natación |
| tennis | el tenis |
| windsurfing | el windsurf |
| volleyball | el voleibol |

## Sports equipment

| | |
|---|---|
| Where can I rent . . . | ¿Dónde puedo alquilar . . .? |
| I'd like to rent . . . | Quiero alquilar . . . |
| a racket | una raqueta |
| some balls | unas pelotas |
| deck chair | una silla de lona |
| fishing rod | una caña |
| fishing net | una red |
| sunshade | una sombrilla |
| golf clubs | unos palos |
| ski boots | unas botas de ski |
| ski poles | unos bastones |
| skis | unos esquís |
| canoe | una canoa |
| dinghy | un bote, un barco |
| sailboat | un velero, un barco de vela |
| sail board | un windsurf |
| wetsuit | un traje de goma |

| | |
|---|---|
| championship | el campeonato |
| game | el juego |
| match, game | el partido |
| round of golf | una vuelta |
| stadium | el estadio |
| swimming pool | la piscina |
| tennis court | la pista de tenis |
| tournament | el torneo |
| track, course | la pista |

# VOCABULARY

## Spanish-English Vocabulary

Note: the letters **ch, ll** and **ñ** are counted as individual letters in Spanish and words beginning with these combinations are listed after **c, l** and **n** respectively.

**a** to, at
**abierto/a** open
**abridor** *m.* bottle opener
**abrir** to open
**abuelo, abuela** grandfather, grandmother.
**acabar** to finish
**accidente** *m.* accident
**aceite** *m.* oil
**aceituna** *f.* olive
**acrílico** *m.* acrylic
**acuerdo: de -** agreed, I agree
**adiós** goodbye
**aduana** *f.* customs
**aeopuerto** *m.* airport
**afición** *f.* hobby
**agencia** *(f)* **de viajes** travel agency
**agradable** pleasant
**agua** water; **- potable** drinking water; **- mineral** mineral water
**agujero** *m.* hole
**ahora** now; **- mismo** this very moment
**ajedrez** *m.* chess
**ajo** *m.* garlic
**albergue** *(m)* **de juventud** youth hostel
**albóndigas** *f.pl.* meatballs
**alcázar** *m.* Moorish castle
**alegre** happy
**alérgico** allergic
**algo** something; **¿ - más?** anything else?
**algodón** *m.* cotton
**algún, alguno** some, any
**almacén** *m.* store; **los grandes almacenes** department store
**almeja** *f.* clam
**almorzar** to have lunch
**almuerzo** *m.* lunch
**aquilar** to rent
**alquiler** *(m)* **de coches** car rental
**alto/a** tall, high
**amable** kind, nice
**ambulancia** *f.* ambulance
**amigo** *m.* **amiga** *f.* friend
**ancho/a** wide
**anchoa** *f.* anchovy
**andar** to walk; **andando** walking
**andén** *m.* platform
**anticiclón** *m.* anticyclone
**año** *m.* year

**aparatos eléctricos** *m. pl.* electric appliances
**aparcamiento** *m.* parking space, parking lot
**aparcar** to park
**apellido** *m.* surname
**aquí** here
**arrancar** to start (a car)
**arreglar** to fix, mend
**artículo** *m.* article
**asiento** *m.* seat
**autobús** *m.* bus
**autocar** *m.* intercity bus
**autopista** *f.* freeway
**avería** *f.* breakdown
**averiado** broken (down)
**avión** *m.* airplane
**ayer** yesterday
**ayudar** to help
**ayuntamiento** *m.* town hall
**azúcar** *m.* sugar
**azul** blue

**bailar** to dance
**bajar** to go down, get down
**bajo/a** low, short; under
**balcón** *m.* balcony
**banco** *m.* bank
**bañarse** to bathe, take a bath
**baño** *m.* bathroom; bath
**bar** *m.* bar
**barato/a** cheap
**barca** *(f)* **de vela** sailboat
**barco** *m.* ship
**barra** *f.* bar, counter (inside bar)
**bastante** quite; enough
**batido** *m.* milkshake
**beber** to drink
**bebida** *f.* drink
**biblioteca** *f.* library
**bien** well
**billete** *m.* bill *(currency);* ticket; **-de ida y vuelta** round-trip ticket
**bistec** *m.* steak
**blanco/a** white
**boca** *f.* mouth
**bocadillo** *m.* sandwich
**bodega** *f.* wine cellar
**bolso** *m.* handbag

# VOCABULARY

bonito/a pretty
borrasca f. low-pressure area
botella f. bottle
buen, bueno/a good well; buenos días good morning; buenas tardes good afternoon
buscar to look for

cabeza f. head
cabina telefónica f. telephone booth
cada each
café m. coffee; - con leche coffee and milk; -solo black coffee
cafetería f. café
caja f. cashier; box
cala f. cove
calamar m. squid
caliente hot
calor m. heat; tengo - I am hot
calle f. street
cama f. bed; - matrimonial double bed
cámara f. camera
camarero m. waiter
cambiar to change
cambio m. change; currency exchange
camino m. way, road
camión m. truck
camisa f. shirt
camiseta f. t-shirt
camping m. campsite
caravana f. van
carne f. meat
carnet (m) de identidad identity card
carnicería f. butcher shop
caro/a expensive
carretera f. road, highway
carta f. menu; letter
cartelera f. entertainment page
casa f. house
casado/a married
castillo m. castle
catedral f. cathedral
caza f. shooting, hunting
ceda el paso give way; yield
cena f. dinner, supper
cenar to have dinner
centro m. center; - ciudad downtown
cepillo (m) de dientes toothbrush
cerca (de) near to
cercano near
cerdo m. pork
cerilla f. match
cerrado/a shut

cerrar to shut
cerveza f. beer
cheque (m) viajero traveler's check
cielo m. sky
cigarrillo m. cigarette
cine m. movie theater
cinturón (m) de seguridad seatbelt
circo m. circus
cita f. appointment
ciudad f. city
claro certainly, of course; light (adj)
cobro revertido m. collect call
cocina f. kitchen
coche m. car; coach (of train); - cama sleeping car; - litera berth
coger to take, catch
coja take (from coger)
colegio m. school
color m. color
collar m. necklace
comedor m. dining room
comer to eat
comida f. meal, lunch
como how, ask, like
¿cómo? how? what?
cómodo/a comfortable
completo/a full
comprar to buy
comprender to understand
compresa f. sanitary napkin
comprimido m. pill
computadora f. computer
con with
conejo m. rabbit
conocer to know (person or place)
consigna f. left luggage
controlar to check
coñac m. brandy
copa f. cup; tomar una - to have a drink
cordero m. lamb
correos post office
correspondencia f. connection (train)
corrida f. bullfight
corriente f. current (electric)
corto/a short
costa f. coast
costar to cost
crédito m. credit; tarjeta de - credit card; carta de - letter of credit
crema (f) de tomate tomato soup
cruce m. crossroads
cruzar to cross; cruzca cross over

# VOCABULARY

¿cuál? which?

¿cuándo? when?

¿cuánto(s)?, ¿cuánta(s)? how much? how many?

cuarto *m.* room; - de dormir bedroom; - de estar living room; - de baño bathroom

cuarto *m.* quarter; - de hora quarter of an hour; - de kilo quarter of a kilo

cubierto *m.* cover charge; overcast (adj)

cubo *(m)* de basura trash bin

cuchara *f.* spoon; -da spoonful

cuchillo *m.* knife

cuenta *f.* bill; account; darse - de to realize

cuesta, cuestan it costs, they cost (from costar)

cueva *f.* cave

¡cuidado! careful!

champiñón *m.* mushroom

champú *m.* shampoo

chaqueta *f.* jacket

chica *f.* girl

chico *m.* boy

chocolate *m.* chocolate

choque *m.* collision

chorizo *m.* spicy sausage

chubasco *m.* shower (rain)

chuleta *f.* chop

dar to give; dame, deme give me

deber to owe

decir to say

dejar to leave

delante (de) in front (of)

delgado/a slim, thin

demasiado too, too much

deme give me (from dar)

dentista *m/f.* dentist

dentro (de) within

dependiente/a *m/f.* store clerk

deporte *m.* sport

derecha *f.* right; a la - on/to the right

derecho: todo - straight ahead

desayuno *m.* breakfast

descuento *m.* discount

desde since

desear to want

despacio: ir más - to slow down

despacho *m.* office; - de billetes ticket/office

despejado clear (sky)

después (de) afterwards, after

destino *m.* destination

desviación *f.* detour

detrás (de) behind

devuelve cambio gives change (from devolver to give back)

día *m.* day

diabético/a diabetic

diarrea *f.* diarrhea

diccionario *m.* dictionary

diente *m.* tooth; - de ajo clove of garlic

¡diga! ¡dígame! hello! (on telephone)

dinero *m.* money

dirección *f.* direction; - única one-way street; address

directo direct

disco *m.* record, disc

discoteca *f.* discotheque

divertirse to enjoy oneself

doblar to turn; doble a la derecha turn right

doble double

docena *f.* dozen

doctor *m.* doctor

doler to hurt, have a pain

domicilio *m.* residence

domingo Sunday

¿dónde? where?

dormir to sleep

ducha *f.* shower

duro *m.* 5-peseta coin

edificio *m.* building

el the (masc)

él, ella, he, she; him, her

electricidad *f.* electricity

ellos, ellas they; them

embarazada pregnant

empezar to begin

empresa *f.* company, firm

empujar to push

en in, on

encantar to delight

encender to light

encontrar to meet

enfermera *f.* nurse

enfermo/a ill

enfrente (de) opposite

ensaimada *f.* roll

ensalada *f.* salad

enseñar to show

entender to understand

entonces well, then

# VOCABULARY

entrada *f.* entrance; entrance ticket; hors d'oeuvres
entregar to hand over; **entrega de equipajes** baggage check-in
enviar to send
equipaje *m.* luggage
equipo *m.* team
equitación *f.* horse-riding
**es** he, she, it is, you are (formal)
escalera *f.* staircase
escaparse to run away
escocés, escocesa Scottish
escuchar to listen
**ese, esa** that; **esos, esas** those; **eso** (neuter) that (pronoun)
eso that; **a eso de** about
español, española Spanish
esparadrapo *m.* band-aid
espárragos *m.pl.* asparagus
esposa *f.* wife
esquí *m.* ski; skiing; - **acuático** waterskiing
**esta** this, **estas** these (fem); **ésta** this (one); **éstas** these (ones)
estación *f.* station; - **de ferrocarril** railway station; - **de servicio** service station; - **de autobuses** bus station
estacionamiento *m.* parking
estadio *m.* stadium
estanco *m.* tobacco shop
estar to be
estatua *f.* statue
**este** this; **estos** these (masc); **éste** this (one); **éstos** these (ones)
estilo *m.* style
esto *(neuter)* this (pronoun)
estómago *m.* stomach
estrecho/a narrow, tight
estudiante *m/f.* student
estupendo/a great!
examen *m.* examination
excursión *f.* excursion
exposición *f.* exhibition
expreso *m.* express train
extranjero/a foreign; **al** - abroad

fábrica *f.* factory
falda *f.* skirt
farmacia *f.* pharmacy
fecha *f.* date
ferretería *f.* hardware store
ferrocarril *m.* railway

festivos: días - public holidays
ficha *f.* form
fideos *m.pl.* pasta (vermicelli, etc.)
fiebre *f.* fever; - **del heno** hay fever
fiesta *f.* festival, party
fila *f.* row
filete *m.* fillet
final: al - at the end
firma *f.* signature
firmar to sign
flan *m.* caramel custard
flauta *f.* flute
folleto *m.* brochure
formulario *m.* form
foto *f.* photograph
fresa *f.* strawberry
fresco/a cool
frío/a cool
frito/a fried
fruta *f.* fruit
frutería *f.* fruit store
fumar to smoke; **(no) fumador** (non) smoker
funcionar to work, **no funciona** it is not working
funcionario/a civil servant
fútbol *m.* soccer

gafas *f.pl.* glasses; - **de sol** sunglasses
galés, galesa Welsh
galleta *f.* biscuit, cracker; cookie
gamba *f.* prawn
ganas: tener - de to want to
garaje *m.* garage
gas: con - fizzy; sin - still (of drinks)
gaseosa *f.* fizzy drink
gasóleo *m.* diesel
gasolina *f.* gasoline
gasolinera *f.* gas station
gazpacho *m.* cold soup
gente *f.* people
gordo/a fat
gracias thank you
gramo *m.* gram
grande big; **los grandes almacenes** department stores
grave serious
grifo *m.* tap (faucet)
gripe *f.* influenza
gris grey
guapo/a handsome, pretty
guía *f.* guide-book; *m/f.* guide
guisantes *m.pl.* peas

# VOCABULARY

**guitarra** *f.* guitar
**gustar** to like; **me gusta** I like

**habitación** *f.* room; **- doble** double room; **- individual/sencilla** single room
**hablar** to speak
**hacer** to do; to make; **hace dos años** two years ago; **hace sol** it is sunny; **hace frío/calor** it is cold/hot
**hacia** towards
**hambre** *f.* hunger; **tengo -** I am hungry
**hamburguesa** *f.* hamburger
**hasta** until
**hay** there is, there are; **- que** one must
**helado** *m.* ice cream
**herido/a** hurt
**hermano/a** *m/f.* brother/sister
**hielo** *m.* ice
**hígado** *m.* liver
**hijo/a** *m/f.* son/daughter
**hoguera** *f.* bonfire
**hola** hello
**hombre** *m.* man
**hora** *f.* hour, time
**horario** *m.* timetable, schedule
**hospital** *m.* hospital
**hostal** *m.* family hotel
**hotel** *m.* hotel
**hoy** today
**huevo** *m.* egg

**ida** one-way (ticket) **- y vuelta** round trip
**idioma** *m.* language
**iglesia** *f.* church
**importa: no -** it doesn't matter
**incluido/a** included
**información** *f.* information
**ingeniero** *m.* engineer
**inglés, inglesa** English
**insolación** *f.* sunstroke
**interesar** to interest; **-se** to be interested (in)
**invierno** *m.* winter
**ir** to go; **-se** to go away, leave
**isla** *f.* island
**izquierda** *f.* left; **a la -** on/to the left

**jabón** *m.* soap
**jamón** *m.* ham
**jardín** *m.* garden
**jerez** *m.* sherry
**jersey** *m.* pullover
**juego** *m.* game

**jueves** *m.* Thursday
**jugar** to play (game)
**juguetería** *f.* toy store

**kilo** *m.* kilogram
**kilómetro** *m.* kilometer

**la, las** the (feminine)
**lado** *m.* side; **al otro -** on the other side; **al - de** beside
**lana** *f.* wool
**largo/a** long
**lástima** *f.* **:¡Qué - !** What a pity!
**lata** *f.* tin; can
**lavabo** *m.* basin, washbasin
**lavar** to wash
**leche** *f.* milk
**lechería** *f.* dairy
**leer** to read
**legumbres** *f.pl.* vegetables, beans
**lejos** far; **- de** far from
**lenguado** *m.* sole
**lentillas** *f.pl.* contact lenses
**lento** slowly
**levantarse** to get up
**libra** *f.* pound
**libre** free, vacant
**librería** *f.* bookstore
**libro** *m.* book
**limón** *m.* lemon
**limonada** *f.* lemonade
**línea** *f.* line
**liquidación** *f.* clearance sale
**lista** *f.* list; **- de vinos** wine list
**litro** *m.* liter
**localidad** *f.* seat, ticket
**lugar** *m.* place
**lunes** *m.* Monday

**llamar** to call, telephone; **-se** to be called
**llave** *f.* key
**llegadas** *f.pl.* arrivals
**llegar** to arrive
**llenar** to fill out; fill up
**lleno/a** full
**llevar** to buy, to take; to wear
**llover** to rain; **llueve** it is raining
**lluvia** *f.* rain

**macarrones** *m.* macaroni
**madre** *f.* mother
**maduro/a** ripe

# VOCABULARY

**mal, malo/a** bad
**maleta** *f.* suitcase
**manchego/a** from La Mancha
**mandar** to send
**mantequilla** *f.* butter
**manzana** *f.* apple
**mañana** *f.* morning; tomorrow; **- por la -** tomorrow morning
**mapa** *m.* map
**mar** *m/f.* sea; **- arbolada** very rough sea
**maravilloso/a** wonderful
**marca** *f.* make (of car)
**marcar** to dial (a number)
**mareado/a** faint, dizzy
**marido** *m.* husband
**mariscos** *m.pl.* shellfish
**martes** *m.* Tuesday
**más** more
**matrícula** *f.* number (registration)
**me** me
**mecánico** *m.* mechanic
**medias** *f.pl.* stockings
**médico** *m.* doctor
**medio/a** half, **mediodía** noon, **medianoche** midnight; **y media** half past
**mejillones** *m.pl.* mussels
**mejorarse** to get better
**melocotón** *m.* peach
**menos** less
**menú** *m.* fixed price meal; menu
**mercado** *m.* market
**merienda** *f.* snack
**merluza** *f.* hake (codfish)
**mermelada** *f.* jam
**mes** *m.* month
**mesa** *f.* table
**meter** to put, insert
**metro** *m.* metro, subway, meter
**mezquita** *f.* mosque
**mi, mis** my
**mí** me (emphatic)
**miércoles** *m.* Wednesday
**minuto** *m.* minute
**mirar** to watch, look
**mismo/a** same
**moderno/a** modern
**monasterio** *m.* monastery
**moneda** *f.* coin, change
**monumento** *m.* monument
**mostrar** to show
**mucho** much; **muchísimo** very much
**muebles** *m.pl.* furniture
**mujer** *f.* woman

**multa** *f.* fine
**museo** *m.* museum
**muy** very

**nacionalidad** *f.* nationality
**nada** nothing; **de -** you're welcome; **- más** no more, that's all
**nadar** to swim
**naranja** *f.* orange
**naranjada** *f.* orangeade
**nata** *f.* cream
**natación** *f.* swimming
**necesitar** to need
**negocios: de -** on business
**negro/a** black
**neumático** *m.* tire
**niebla** *f.* fog
**nieve** *f.* snow
**ningún, ninguno/a** none, not any
**niña** *f.* little girl
**niño** *f.* child; little boy
**no** no, not
**noche** *f.* night
**nombre** *m.* name
**normal** regular (gas)
**norte** *m.* north
**nosotros** we, us
**nube** *f.* cloud
**nublado, nuboso** *m.* cloudy
**nuevo/a** new
**número** *m.* number; size (of shoe)

**obra** *f.* work; **obras** roadwork
**ocupado** occupied
**oeste** *m.* west
**oficina** *f.* office
**ojo** *m.* eye
**olvidarse** to forget
**oscuro/a** dark
**otro/a** other, another
**oye** listen (from **oír** to listen)

**padre** *m.* father; **-s** parents
**pagar** to pay
**país** *m.* country
**palacio** *m.* palace
**pan** *m.* bread
**panadería** *f.* bakery
**panecillo** *m.* bread roll
**pantalones** *m.pl.* trousers
**papel** *m.* paper; **-es de seguros** insurance papers

# VOCABULARY

**papelería** *f.* stationery store
**paquete** *m.* packet, package
**par** *m.* pair
**para** to, for
**parada** *f.* bus stop
**parar** to stop
**parecer** to seem; **me parece que** I think that
**parque** *m.* park
**partido** *m.* match (soccer)
**pasado/a** previous, last; **la semana pasada** last week
**pasaporte** *m.* passport
**pasar** to spend (time); to pass; to happen
**pasear** to go for a walk
**paseo** *m.* walk; broad avenue
**paso** *m.* way
**pasta** *(f)* **de dientes** toothpaste
**pastel** *m.* pastry, cake
**pastelería** *f.* pastry shop
**pastilla** *f.* lozenge
**patata** *f.* potato
**peaje** *m.* toll
**peatones** *m.pl.* pedestrians
**película** *f.* film (in movies, etc.)
**peligro** *m.* danger
**pelo** *m.* hair
**peluquería** *f.* hairdresser
**pensar** to think
**pensión** *f.* boardinghouse; board; - **completa** full board; - **media** half board
**pequeño/a** small
**pera** *f.* pear
**perdón** pardon, excuse me
**perfume** *m.* perfume
**perfumería** *f.* cosmetics shop
**periódico** *m.* newspaper
**periodista** *m/f.* journalist
**permiso** *(m)* **de conducir** driver's license
**persona** *f.*person
**pesca** *f.* fishing
**pescadería** *f.* fish store
**pescado** *m.* fish
**peseta** *f.* peseta (unit of currency)
**picadura** *f.* sting
**picar** to sting
**pie** *m.* foot; **a** - on foot
**pila** *f.* battery
**píldora** *f.* contraceptive pill
**pimienta** *f.* pepper

**pimiento** *m.* pepper (green, etc.)
**pinchazo** *m.* flat (tire)
**pintura** *f.* painting
**piscina** *f.* swimming pool
**piso** *m.* floor (story); flat (apartment)
**pista** *f.* track, court; - **de tenis** tennis court
**plano** *m.* plan, map
**planta** *(f)* **baja** ground floor
**plátano** *m.* banana
**plato** *m.* plate, dish; - **combinado** meal on one plate
**playa** *f.* beach
**plaza** *f.* square; seat; - **de toros** bullring; **plazas libres** vacant seats
**plomo** *m.*lead
**poco** little, a little
**poder** to be able
**policía** *f.* police; *m.* police officer
**pollo** *m.* chicken
**poner** to put; to show (a film); **póngame** give me
**por** for, through, during, along; - **favor** please; - **aquí** this way; ¿**por qué?** why?
**porque** because
**porrón** *m.* glass wine container
**postal** *f.* postcard
**postre** *m.* dessert
**practicar** to practice
**precio** *m.* price
**preferir** to prefer
**prefijo** *m.* area code (telephone)
**preocuparse** to worry
**presentar** to introduce
**presión** *f.* pressure
**primavera** *f.* spring
**primer, primero/a** first
**primo** *m.*, **prima** *f.* cousin
**principios: a** - **de** at the beginning (of)
**probador** *m.* fitting room
**probarse** to try on
**profesor** *m.*, **profesora** *f.* teacher
**profundo/a** deep
**prohibido** forbidden
**pronóstico** *m.* forecast
**propina** *f.* tip
**próximo/a** next
**puede: ¿se puede?** can one?
**puente** *m.* bridge
**puerta** *f.* door
**puerto** *m.* port
**puesto** *(m)* **de socorro** first-aid station

# VOCABULARY

**que** what, that, than; **¿qué?** what? which? how?; **¿qué tal?** how are you? (informal)

**quedar** to keep, be left; **quedarse** to stay, remain

**querer** to want; **quiero** I want

**queso** *m.* cheese

**¿quién?** who?

**quiosco** *m.* newsstand

**quisiera** I would like

**quizás** perhaps

**ración** *f.* portion

**rápido** *m.* fast train

**rato: un -** a while

**rebajas** *f.pl.* bargains

**recado** *m.* message

**recepción** *f.* reception

**receta** *f.* prescription

**recogida** *(f)* **de equipajes** baggage claim

**reducción** *f.* reduction

**refresco** *m.* soft drink

**reloj** *m.* watch, clock

**reparar** to repair

**reserva** *f.* reservation

**reservar** to reserve

**resfriado** *m.* cold, flu

**residencia** *f.* guest house

**respirar** to breathe

**restaurante** *m.* restaurant

**resto** *m.* remainder

**retraso** *m.* delay

**revista** *f.* magazine

**río** *m.* river

**robar** to steal

**roca** *f.* rock

**rodaja** *f.* slice

**rojo/a** red

**ropa** *f.* clothes

**rubio/a** *m.* blonde

**sábado** Saturday

**saber** to know

**sacacorchos** *m.* corkscrew

**sacar** to take out, get (tickets)

**saco** *(m)* **de dormir** sleeping bag

**sal** *f.* salt

**sala** *(f)* **de espera** waiting room

**salchichas** *f.pl.* sausages

**salchichón** *m.* sausage

**salida** *f.* exit; **salidas** departures

**salsa** *(f)* **de tomate** tomato sauce

**sándwich** *(m)* **caliente** toasted sandwich

**sangría** *f.* red wine

**secretaria** *f.* secretary

**seda** *f.* silk

**seguida: en -** at once

**seguir** to follow, continue

**segundo/a** second; **de -** for the second course

**seguro** *m.* insurance; sure (adj)

**sello** *m.* stamp

**semana** *f.* week

**sentar** to fit, suit; **-se** to sit

**sentirse** to feel, **lo siento** I'm sorry

**señor** Mr., gentleman

**señorita** Miss, young lady

**señora** Mrs., lady

**ser** to be

**serio** serious

**servicio** *m.* service; **-s** toilets

**sesión** *(f)* **continua** continuous performance

**si** if

**sí** yes

**siempre** always

**¡siga!** follow! (from **seguir**)

**simpático/a** nice, pleasant

**sin** without

**sitio** *m.* place, site

**sobre** above, over; **- todo** especially

**sol** *m.* sun, **hace -** it is sunny

**solo** only; **café -** black coffee

**soltero/a** single (unmarried)

**sombrero** *m.* hat

**somnífero** *m.* sleeping pill

**sopa** *f.* soup

**su** his, her, its, their; your

**subir** to go up, climb

**suéter** *m.* sweater

**super** premium (gas)

**supermercado** *m.* supermarket

**suplemento** *m.* surcharge

**sur** *m.* south

**tabla** *(f)* **a vela** windsurfer

**tacón** *m.* heel

**tal** such; **¿qué tal?** how are you?

**talla** *f.* size

**taller mecánico** *m.* workshop, garage

**también** also

**tapas** *f.pl.* appetizers

**taquilla** *f.* ticket window

**tardar** to delay, to take time

**tarde** *f.* afternoon, early evening; late

# VOCABULARY

**tarjeta** *f.* card; **- postal** postcard; **tarjeta de crédito** credit card
**tarta** *f.* tart, cake
**taxi** *m.* taxi
**taza** *f.* cup
**té** *m.* tea
**teatro** *m.* theater
**teléfono** *m.* telephone
**televisor** *m.* television set
**temperatura** *f.* temperature
**templado/a** mild
**temporal** *m.* gale, storm
**tenderse** to lie down
**tenedor** *m.* fork
**tener** to have; **tengo hambre/sed** I am hungry/thirsty; **tengo veinte años** I am twenty years old
**tenis** *m.* tennis
**terminar** to finish; **terminado** finished
**ternera** *f.* veal
**terraza** *f.* terrace, balcony
**tiempo** *m.* weather
**tienda** *f.* store; **- de campaña** tent
**tierra** *f.* land
**tinto** *m.* red wine
**tirita** *f.* bandage
**toalla** *f.* towel; **-de baño** bathtowel
**tocar** to play (instrument)
**todo** all, every; everything; **- derecho** straight ahead
**tomar** to take; **-una copa** to have a drink
**tomate** *m.* tomato
**tormenta** *f.* thunderstorm
**toro** *m.* bull
**tortilla** *f.* omelette
**tos** *f.* cough
**tostada** *f.* toast
**trabajar** to work
**trabajo** *m.* work, job
**traer** to bring; **¡traiga!** bring!
**traje** *m.* suit; **- de baño** bathing suit
**transbordo** *m.* change, transfer
**transeúnte** *m.* passerby
**tren** *m.* train; **-es de cercanías** local trains; **-es de largo recorrido** long-distance trains
**triste** sad
**trozo** *m.* piece
**tu** your (informal)
**tú** you (informal)
**turismo** *m.* tourism
**turista** *m/f.* tourist

**último/a** last
**un, uno/una** a; one; **unos/unas** some
**usted/ustedes** you (formal)

**vacaciones** *f.pl.* vacation; **de -** on vacation
**vainilla** *f.* vanilla
**¡vale!** OK!
**valer** to cost, to be worth
**valor** *m.* value
**valle** *m.* valley
**vamos** let's go
**vaqueros** *m.pl.* jeans
**vaso** *m.* glass
**vendedor** *m.,* **vendedora** *f.* sales assistant
**venir** to come; **¡venga!** come here!
**venta** *f.* sale; **-anticipada** advance sales
**ventana** *f.* window
**ver** to see; **a -** let's see
**verano** *m.* summer
**¿verdad?** isn't it? aren't you? don't you?
**verde** green
**verdulería** *f.* produce store
**verduras** *f.pl.* vegetables
**vermut** *m.* vermouth
**vestido** *m.* dress
**vez** *f.* time; **una -** once; **dos veces** twice
**vía** *f.* track, platform
**viajar** to travel
**viaje** *m.* journey
**viejo/a** old
**viento** *m.* wind
**viernes** *m.* Friday
**vinagre** *m.* vinegar
**vino** *m.* wine
**visitar** to visit
**vista** *f.* view; **- del mar** sea view; **hasta la -** till we meet again
**vivir** to live
**volver** to return
**vosotros** you (plural)
**vuelo** *m.* flight
**vuelta** *f.* change; walk

**y** and
**ya** already
**yo** I

**zapatería** *f.* shoe store
**zapatos** *m.pl.* shoes
**zumo** *m.* juice